WHAT YOUR COLLEAGUES ARE SAYING . . .

Fisher, Frey, Smith, and Hattie have provided a practical, user-friendly playbook that supports school leaders as they strive to leverage their leadership skills in what is called the "new normal." My main take-away from this playbook is that the ideas within these pages will enhance instructional leadership well beyond distance learning and allow school leaders to extend the reach of their impact to any setting at any time. This playbook will enhance leading for engagement and impact for years to come.

> John Almarode, Associate Professor and Executive
> Director of Teaching and Learning
> College of Education, James Madison University
> Co-Author, *Great Teaching by Design* and
> *The Distance Learning Playbook for College and University Instruction*
> Waynesboro, VA

Learning *can* happen from a distance—especially when leaders support teachers, students, and parents, also from a distance. This essential guide offers practical steps for leaders to foster a sense of community and lead professional learning with teachers. With resources like this, we just might all emerge from this crisis as *better* educators than we were before.

> Julie Stern, International Consultant and Educator
> Author*, Tools for Teaching Conceptual Understanding,*
> *Learning That Transfers,* and *Visible Learning® for Social Studies*
> Washington, DC

The Distance Learning Playbook for School Leaders is an essential companion for any leader who is looking for measured, actionable, and practical insights. Fisher, Frey, Smith, and Hattie have created a resource that supports leaders as they navigate through the uncharted territory of leading from a distance.

> Vince Bustamante, Consultant and Instructional Coach
> Co-Author, *Great Teaching by Design*
> Edmonton, AB, Canada

In this time of uncertainty and continual change, *The Distance Learning Playbook for School Leaders* provides educational leaders a practical yet profound framework on how to reflect, understand, and act on the effective practices that uniquely tie together our students, our teachers, and ourselves to collectively achieve optimal outcomes. The practical tools provided throughout this book make it accessible and actionable for all readers.

> Joseph Jones, Superintendent
> New Castle County Vo-Tech School District
> Wilmington, DE

With *The Distance Learning Playbook for School Leaders,* Fisher, Frey, Smith and Hattie have created an accessible and thorough guide for educators addressing the complex needs of all members of their school communities in the time of the COVID-19 pandemic. This book arrives just in time to be an invaluable resource for educators and school communities across the country looking to uphold high standards for teaching and provide students with quality educational experiences, even when it is at a distance.

Martha Staeheli, Instructor
Program for Recovery and Community Health
Yale School of Medicine Department of Psychiatry
New Haven, CT

Most leadership books tell you how to work harder or more efficiently, without acknowledging the mental health burden school leadership often takes. What's refreshing in this book is that it starts with individual self-care and self-care for your colleagues. I intend to use the planning frameworks the authors suggested in order to ensure self-care is prioritized for myself and my colleagues at my school site.

Courtney Miller, Assistant Principal
California School of the Arts, San Gabriel Valley
Culturally Responsive Teaching and Restorative
Practices Consultant, Inclusive Teacher Academy
Covina, CA

Both a guidebook and reflective workbook in one, *The Distance Learning Playbook for School Leaders* coaches you to lead successful distance learning with all stakeholders in mind. Each segment identifies clear goals and guiding questions for you to consider in your own context, so you can address the needs of your staff, students, and parents. This is a must-read for any school leader who wants to empower their teams to respond to new challenges and shape an effective distance learning environment.

Janine Slaga, Head of Primary Music
United World College of South East Asia
Singapore

In these tumultuous times, effective leadership is critical. This book provides a compelling view into the complex art of leading schools today. This is an invaluable book for any school leader who seeks to be balanced, wise, and engaged with all stakeholders.

Fatma Trabelsi, Independent Educational Consultant
Association of International Educators and Leaders of Color
Tunis, Tunisia

With school systems now consigned to an online learning model as a response to the ongoing pandemic, school leaders need to deeply consider how to lead learning from a distance. *The Distance Learning Playbook for School Leaders* provides practical strategies, rubrics, surveys, and activities to address the problems faced in the new "normal." Utilizing essential questions paired with a strategic goal, the authors enter the world of school leadership and provide actionable insights. For any administrator seeking a hands-on guide to maximize their impact and increase engagement in uncertain and complex settings, this book is your must-have, go-to resource.

Megel Barker, MYP Coordinator
Assistant Principal
ABA Oman International School
Muscat, Oman

Adjusting to the present norm effectively is a major concern for most educators. *The Distance Learning Playbook for School Leaders* is a timely and relevant guide for leaders on how to carry out their roles virtually without compromising standards and expectations. Leaders will learn how every stakeholder's—including parents, families, communities, and teachers—interests can be fully protected in an online learning environment.

Ngozi Umoru, Educator
Association of International Educators and Leaders of Color
Lagos, Nigeria

In our lifetime we have not had to consider how to lead schools during a worldwide crisis. *The Distance Learning Playbook for School Leaders* reminds us that what teachers and leaders do is really what matters, not the medium which they do it through. With the right skills and attitude, this timely playbook offers excellent tips and reminders that can easily guide school leaders on every level through crisis and into a strong climate of excellence.

Zetha Nobles, International School Leader
Chief Strategist, Nobles Global Consultants
Cypress, TX

Timely advice for leadership teams to make instructional leadership a priority by providing opportunities, guidance and explicit action steps to increase administrator and teacher agency. No longer is teacher self-care, accountability partnerships, and applying safe practices before implementation taking a back seat; *The Distance Learning Playbook for School Leaders* shares how to set the foundation for supporting teachers, families, and students in this rapid transition to online teaching and learning through easy to apply research-based strategies. A must read for school district and K–12 administrators.

Dr. Sonja Lopez Arnak, Faculty in Teacher Education
Alliant International University
Teach-Now/Moreland University
Washington, DC

This is a great practical guide for managing both the stress and priorities associated with distance learning. As a new school leader navigating my way through principalship, this book references many obstacles that I have already faced in the first month of school and challenges that have presented itself along the way. The section on virtual learning walks really hit home because my district heavily focuses on this practice, so I was able to make meaningful connections. Also, the reflective guides embedded in the book give me useful tools to implement in either my leadership team meetings or schoolwide faculty meetings.

Amanda Austin, Director
Iberville STEM Academy
Addis, LA

This book is insightful, progressive, and just what school leaders need to move their organizations forward. Due to the COVID-19 pandemic, the field of education was forced to shift its ethos on a dime. This guide to distance learning will support the nimbleness and flexibility needed to create and implement and sustain a high-quality distance learning program with fidelity.

Mona Fairley-Nelson, Deputy Head of School,
Curriculum, Instruction, and Assessment
Carol Morgan School
Santo Domingo, Dominican Republic

This is the book school leaders need to be reading right now. *The Distance Learning Playbook for School Leaders* provides just-in-time support while also being timeless in nature. The authors tackle the very things we are wrestling with in a highly relatable and action-oriented way.

Brad Gustafson
National Distinguished Principal and Best-Selling Author
St. Michael, MN

As schools transition into a new way of operating, *The Distance Learning Playbook for School Leaders* helps us to dot our I's and cross our T's as we move into learning, leading, and continuously growing in a virtual setting. Not only does the playbook ensure a well-rounded view of our current situation, it provides leaders an opportunity to pause and carefully develop plans of action based on guided reflection. This book will enable leaders to persevere through today's challenges and keep the focus on student learning.

Connie Hamilton, Speaker and Education Consultant
Author, *Hacking Questions and Hacking Homework*
Detroit, MI

THE

DISTANCE LEARNING PLAYBOOK FOR

SCHOOL LEADERS

THE
DISTANCE
LEARNING
PLAYBOOK FOR
SCHOOL LEADERS

LEADING FOR ENGAGEMENT
AND IMPACT IN ANY SETTING

**DOUGLAS FISHER · NANCY FREY
DOMINIQUE SMITH · JOHN HATTIE**

CORWIN

FOR INFORMATION:

Corwin

A SAGE Company

2455 Teller Road

Thousand Oaks, California 91320

(800) 233-9936

www.corwin.com

SAGE Publications Ltd.

1 Oliver's Yard

55 City Road

London EC1Y 1SP

United Kingdom

SAGE Publications India Pvt. Ltd.

B 1/I 1 Mohan Cooperative Industrial Area

Mathura Road, New Delhi 110 044

India

SAGE Publications Asia-Pacific Pte. Ltd.

18 Cross Street #10-10/11/12

China Square Central

Singapore 048423

Acquisitions Editor: Ariel Curry

Associate Content Development Editor: Jessica Vidal

Production Editor: Melanie Birdsall

Copy Editor: Diane DiMura

Typesetter: C&M Digitals (P) Ltd.

Proofreader: Susan Schon

Indexer: Sheila Hill

Cover Designer: Gail Buschman

Marketing Manager: Charline Maher

Section-opening images courtesy of iStock.com/Eoneren

Printed in the United States of America

ISBN 9781071839843

Library of Congress Control Number: 2020917767

This book is printed on acid-free paper.

20 21 22 23 24 10 9 8 7 6 5 4 3 2

CONTENTS

MINDFRAMES FOR LEADERS FROM A DISTANCE 91

Visit the companion website at
resources.corwin.com/DLPlaybook-leaders
for downloadable resources.

INTRODUCTION

In March 2020, there was no manual for leading schools and school systems during a pandemic. Instead, leaders across the world worked to figure things out as the crisis unfolded. Collectively, we made a number of good decisions and some that were not so good. But we developed knowledge, sometimes through trial and error and sometimes based on evidence and experience from the past. There is not a lot of information about supporting and guiding the learning process when our teachers and students were not physically present in our buildings. Teacher leaders, site administrators, and central office leaders all engaged in learning to ensure that schools still delivered on their promises to provide quality learning experiences for students. And this book is for everyone involved in the leadership of schools.

When schools shifted to digital in a matter of days, leaders' first worries were equity related. Did students have access to technology? Did they have food? Did they have support for learning? Slowly, we moved to ensuring that the instructional experiences were sound. And we worked to maintain the well-being of the staff and students. We realized that we need to increase teachers' access to professional learning and that new instructional frameworks would be required. It's really quite impressive, the amount of information that has been collected about leading schools from a distance. In fact, this book is based on the lessons learned from eighteen schools whose leaders shared their experiences with us. This book is also based on the vast **Visible Learning**® research collection (www.visiblelearningmetax.com). For those of you unfamiliar with the Visible Learning research, John Hattie has been collecting meta-analyses for many years. At this point, there are over 1,800 of them.

Meta-analyses are collections of studies, sometimes hundreds of them, that allow researchers to determine an effect size, or the overall magnitude of a specific action, intervention, or influence. For example, boredom has an effect size of −0.47. In other words, a very significant negative influence on learning. Compare that with teaching vocabulary, which has an effect size of 0.63, a pretty strong influence on learning (Figure 0.1). We use the Visible Learning database to make some of the recommendations in this book. For others, we draw on the experiences of leaders who have evidence of their impact during distance learning.

This brings us to the effect size of distance learning itself. We know the effect size of technology remains low and has been so for the last fifty years.

DISTANCE LEARNING IS NOT AN ACCELERATOR OR OBSTACLE OF LEARNING. WHAT TEACHERS AND LEADERS *DO* MATTERS, NOT THE MEDIUM IN WHICH THEY DO IT.

Figure 0.1 Visible Learning Barometer

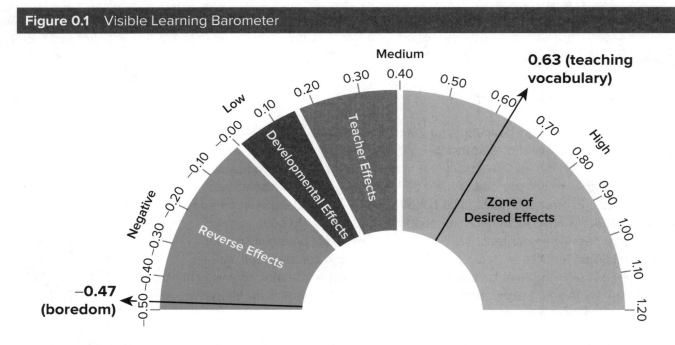

As Dylan Wiliam has often said, technology is the revolution that is still coming! The effect of distance learning is small (0.17) but that does not mean it is NOT effective. In fact, the studies on distance learning, which compare learning from a distance to learning in a physical school, indicate that the setting is not the determining factor for learning. That means it does not matter whether teachers undertake teaching in person or from a distance over the internet (or, as when John started in his first university, via the post office). In other words, distance learning is not an accelerator or obstacle of learning. What teachers and leaders *do* matters, not the medium in which they do it.

As Paul Manna (2015) reminded us, leaders can be magnifiers and multipliers of effective instruction. That did not change during distance learning. We still have to engage in instructional leadership. We must ensure that there is a strong climate for learning. We must work to deliver on the promise of equity. Teachers still need opportunities to learn, just like their students. In fact, we may need to accelerate teachers' access to professional learning. Interestingly, professional development programs have an effect size of 0.37, slightly below the average of all influences in the entire Visible Learning database (0.40). Why is that? It's probably obvious to you. So much of the professional learning provided to teachers is "sit and get" or compliance related and does not allow for sustained interaction with ideas. We can change that, if we want.

Although this book will include apps, programs, platforms, and tools, it's not a book about software. Technology tools will change. In fact, there will be new tools out by the time this book is published. Tech tools are not the important thing. They are necessary and teachers need them to do their work from a distance, but as Beaudoin (2015) noted in his article on distance learning leadership, "Manage change rather than technology" (p. 36). That's what this book is about. And that's the reason we end this book with a focus on the mindframes for leaders. We will adapt the mindframes presented by Hattie and Smith (2021) for distance learning as we believe that practicing these mindframes will serve you well in any instructional setting, well after the pandemic. In doing so, schools will come back better than they were before.

1 SCHOOL CLIMATE AT A DISTANCE

One of the things you can do as a leader is to establish, maintain, and repair (as needed) the climate of the school. Part of the role of the leader is to nurture a school climate to become one that is supportive of learning. This includes the experiences of the staff and students. One challenge with distance learning is that students and staff can fail to feel part of something larger. When that happens, people feel isolated and wonder if their efforts are valuable. Leaders who maintain the climate of their school from a distance create a place where people feel that they belong and thus they work together to impact learning.

In this section:

- ☐ TAKE CARE OF YOURSELF
- ☐ TAKE CARE OF YOUR COLLEAGUES
- ☐ LEADER CREDIBILITY
- ☐ INSTRUCTIONAL LEADERSHIP TEAMS
- ☐ STAKEHOLDER ADVISORY GROUPS
- ☐ VIRTUAL VISIBILITY
- ☐ THE FEEL OF SCHOOL

High school principal Luis Pérez and vice-principals Diana Hopkinson and Robert Russo meet first thing each day for a staff check-in. This daily ten-minute morning meeting is for all the adults in the school and was a tradition before the school moved to distance learning because of the COVID-19 pandemic. "We do it online now, but other than that it is very similar to what we have been doing for years," said Dr. Pérez. After morning meeting, Ms. Hopkinson records the daily greeting and announcements that teachers play in their second period class. "These routines help to remind students and staff that we have an identity as a school," she said.

When live session classes begin, each of the administrators visit classrooms virtually. Today, Mr. Russo is visiting the classrooms of the early career teachers. "Our collective goal is to make contact with 10 percent of the staff each day," he explained. "That means that in a two-week time period, every staff member has had contact." After he is finished, he will meet with the advisory team of clerical staff. Later that afternoon, he has an advisory meeting with parents. "We have several different advisories going, and we meet with each of them once a month. Super important right now in distance learning."

Later in the week, the three administrators will conduct a scheduled virtual learning walk with the mathematics and science department heads to monitor how an instructional initiative is going. "I don't know where we'd be without our ILT [instructional leadership team]," said Dr. Pérez. "We've been able to continue to grow as a school despite some obvious limitations." The ILT consists of teacher leaders from across the school, and they advise on professional learning.

Ms. Hopkinson and Mr. Russo each have taken on elements of student connection. They have divided up the virtual student clubs and check in with the faculty advisory and student leadership each month. Mr. Russo oversees the school's Instagram and Twitter accounts with the student social media club. "We spotlight students each day and build our Instagram stories with things students are doing in and out of school." Each of the administrators writes messages that are deployed to specific groups each week using timeline software to schedule their messages. Ms. Hopkinson said, "It helps me to be able to write five quick messages for the week and then schedule them ahead of time. Then I don't have to remember to do it every day. Way better use of time. We want to make sure that our students know that they are part of something special and unique. Even though they're not physically here, they know that they are still hawks and we still care about them."

The terms *culture* and *climate* are often used interchangeably in everyday speech, but they carry a more specific connotation when it comes to organizational health. *Culture* is a product of the of the rules, procedures, and unspoken ways in which school gets "done." But *climate* is how it feels. Climate is the product of the perceptions of those in the organization. Does the school feel welcoming to students and families? Do staff members feel valued? Do teachers feel empowered to make decisions? While there may be processes in place to address all of these, not every stakeholder may describe the climate as being one where they are welcomed, valued, and empowered.

Building a positive school climate in virtual schooling is a special challenge. Without opportunities to connect with staff and students in hallways, classrooms, and common areas, school leaders must be more creative with the tools they have. The climate of any school is not static and of course is subject to change as the year progresses. However, a positive school climate has the potential to accelerate student learning, with an effect size of 0.43 (Hattie, 2020).

Before you move into this section of the playbook, take a few minutes to self-assess where you currently are in building a virtual school climate.

DRAWING ON MY EXPERTISE

Think about the current context of your school during distance learning.
Use the traffic light scale to reflect on your practices as a school leader. To what extent is each of these statements true? If you want to know if your perceptions are shared by teachers, staff, and family members, you can modify these questions and send them out anonymously to compare and potentially make changes.

	1. I have daily interactions with staff.
	2. I maintain my visibility with staff and students.
	3. I have regular two-way communication routines with families.
	4. I seek to promote a unique school identity.
	5. I foster social and emotional learning and wellbeing among staff.
	6. I attend to my credibility as a school leader among staff, students, and families.

TAKE CARE OF YOURSELF

ESSENTIAL QUESTION: Am I attending to my own personal well-being?

YOUR GOAL: Develop a self-care plan and implement it.

Superintendent Francisco Escobedo reminds us that you cannot fill the cup of another if yours is empty. That's an important message and one that has been too often overlooked as leaders lead through a crisis. But burning the candle from both ends, as the saying goes, only works for so long. It's not sustainable. If you take care of yourself, you can lead for the long term.

This is not a self-help book. But we do want to acknowledge that your attitude influences the climate of the school. Teachers and staff members look to their leaders to judge the status of the organization. Lead with confidence. We've got this. Really, we do. Will there be bumps in the road? Of course. But have you ever had a school year without bumps? Refrain from complaining about days gone by when students were physically in school, full-time, interacting in small, close groups with their peers. Instead, acknowledge the efforts to ensure deep learning during a crisis.

But back to you. Your well-being is important. There are only so many things that you can control. And you can control your efforts to maintain your physical and mental well-being.

NOTE TO SELF

MY MORNING ROUTINE OPTIONS	WHEN I WILL TAKE BREAKS	MY END-OF-DAY ROUTINE OPTIONS

Ask yourself the following questions:

- **Do I have a morning routine?** Engaging in some regular routines is relaxing as predictable events reduce stress. Maybe you walk or run in the morning. Maybe you have breakfast with your family. Maybe you listen to music. You used to have a commute to school that allowed you to mentally prepare for the day. Working from home interrupted that. What new ritual are you going to use to replace your commute, to help you prepare mentally?

- **Do I have a dedicated workspace?** Strange as it may sound, having a place that you "go" to work is helpful. It can keep you organized and tell your brain that you are at work. Negotiate with the people in your home to establish guidelines for that environment so that you can reduce conflict.

- **Do I take breaks?** Step away from the computer and phone. Take a break, and not just to use the bathroom or do laundry. We need breaks from computer screens and we need breaks to allow our thinking to settle.

- **Do I eat healthy?** There are all kinds of recommendations for eating, from intermittent fasting to several small meals per day. Do you have a plan and do you stick with it?

- **How do I tell my brain that work is finished for the day?** In the past, you drove away from the building (even if you did some email from home at night). What will you do to tell your brain that work has finished for the day?

- **Am I getting enough sleep?** Sleep is restorative and allows us to consolidate our memories. Put yourself to bed at the same time each night if at all possible. If you have trouble sleeping, you may want to consult a professional. And remember, no screens for the last hour before you sleep.

We are not trying to preach to you about self-care. But we did see a lot of burnout and increased stress during the pandemic teaching of March through May of 2020. Do what you can to take care of yourself. You and your family and friends, not to mention the people you work with, will benefit from your efforts.

MAKE IT ACTIONABLE

Without sounding too touchy-feely, stress, sleep, and healthy eating and exercise habits are important to our well-being. Your turn. What can you do to support your well-being?

IF YOU TAKE CARE OF YOURSELF, YOU CAN LEAD FOR THE LONG TERM.

NOTE TO SELF

My plan for stress management

_____

_____

_____

_____

My plan for healthy eating

_____

_____

_____

_____

_____

My exercise plan

_____

_____

_____

_____

_____

My plan for getting regular sleep

_____

_____

_____

_____

_____

We know that developing a wellness plan is only part of it. Having a commitment partner increases the likelihood that you will actually implement your plans. Teacher Angelica Chavez was very honest about this. As she said, she had a lot of plans in her mind and sometimes they were even written out. But they were rarely implemented. When she learned about the value of commitment partners, she contacted another teacher on her grade level and asked if they could check-in with each other each week. "I knew that I would have to answer to Pam," Ms. Chavez said, "so I would really do it. But it turns out, I really like what I decided to do and was super happy to talk with her and share my success. I don't know what I was waiting for all of those years. If I had only known."

It's your turn. Who could serve as your commitment partner and what would you ask of that person?

My commitment partner is _____

I need the following from this person:

_____

_____

_____

_____

_____

_____

_____

We will check in

☐ Daily

☐ Two times per week

☐ Three times per week

☐ Weekly

☐ Bi-weekly

TAKE CARE OF YOUR COLLEAGUES

ESSENTIAL QUESTION: How am I fostering well-being among the staff?

YOUR GOAL: Support the emotional lives of staff so they can do the same for others.

The difficult events of 2020 have included a global pandemic, protests against racial injustices, and any number of more localized disasters. As members of the community, the adults in the school are experiencing their own personal traumas and dealing with uncertainty at levels most have never before experienced. We have always known the importance of the well-being of the staff to reduce burnout and promote the collective impact of the school. But school leaders are challenged in new ways to ensure that colleagues are supported in ways that promote healing and growth. There isn't one magical answer to doing so. However, having systems in place can create a more effective safety net.

Conduct mindset check-ins at every staff meeting. One of the most effective ways to model the importance of well-being is by demonstrating how much you value it. Each time you get together with staff, invite them to take a few moments to center themselves on the purpose at hand. You might begin with a short breathing exercise or play some energetic music to get everyone out of their chairs and moving (chances are, they've been sitting for too long anyway!). Pose a question that people can discuss in a small group breakout room or respond to in the Chat function:

- What's the kindest thing someone has done for you this week?
- What was the last thing your students taught you?
- If you were a professional wrestler, what would your entrance song be?

As you can see from the range of questions, they should be light, positive, and display a gentle good humor.

Host gatherings so that staff members can stay connected. Don't underestimate the power of socialization for fostering *esprit de corp*. One of the administrators at the school where we work hosts a trivia game immediately after our weekly professional learning. Anyone who would like to can join, and there is no pressure to do so if someone chooses not to. Ask people to submit the make and model of their first car and then challenge the staff to match the vehicle to the owner. A virtual scavenger hunt, a team-based game like Name That Tune—events like these can help colleagues who might otherwise feel isolated.

Conduct private weekly check-ins with staff members. Send a weekly one-question survey (such as the one at the top of page 13) to every staff member asking them to do their own emotional temperature check. You can use a tool such as Google Forms. The responses you receive can help you in rendering guidance or assistance to anyone who needs it.

Please choose one of the following responses: How are you doing this week?

- I am doing well this week in my job and personally.
- I have a challenge in my job this week but have someone to talk to about it.
- I have a challenge personally this week but have someone to talk to about it.
- I'd like to talk with you about something related to my job.
- I'd like to talk with you about something related to my well-being.
- I'm not exactly sure how I'm doing. Can we talk?

MAKE IT ACTIONABLE

In a time of great community stress, educators can experience compassion fatigue. Most of the time, we experience compassion satisfaction, which is the pleasure we derive from being able to do our work well (Stamm, 2010). When we feel effective, especially when we see evidence of our students' learning, our compassion satisfaction increases.

The other side of this coin is compassion fatigue. Compassion fatigue is a combination of physical, emotional, and spiritual depletion associated with the trauma-related work we do where others are in significant emotional pain or physical distress. It's known as the high cost of caring. As Figley (2002) notes, "Compassion fatigue is a state experienced by those helping people in distress; it is an extreme state of tension and preoccupation with the suffering of those being helped to the degree that it can create a secondary traumatic stress for the helper" (p. 1435). As Elliott, Elliott, and Spears (2018) note, "Symptoms can develop over a period of years, or after as little as six weeks on the job. Lowered tolerance for frustration, an aversion to working with certain students, and decreased job satisfaction are just a few of the effects that represent a significant risk to job performance as well as to teachers' own personal, emotional, and physical well-being" (p. 29). The signs of compassion fatigue include the following:

- Isolation
- Emotional outbursts
- Sadness, apathy
- Impulse to rescue anyone in need
- Persistent physical ailments
- Substance abuse
- Hypervigilance or hyperarousal
- Recurring nightmares or flashbacks
- Excessive complaints about colleagues, management, or those being helped

The American Academy of Family Physicians developed a self-assessment tool for health care workers, which we have adapted for educators (see Figure 1.1). If you see signs in a colleague that are of concern to you, reach out and get them connected with school and district resources, including the Employee Assistance Program.

Figure 1.1 Compassion Fatigue Inventory

Personal concerns commonly intrude on my professional role.	Yes	No
My colleagues seem to lack understanding.	Yes	No
I find even small changes enormously draining.	Yes	No
I can't seem to recover quickly after association with trauma.	Yes	No
Association with trauma affects me very deeply.	Yes	No
My students' stress affects me deeply.	Yes	No
I have lost my sense of hopefulness.	Yes	No
I feel vulnerable all the time.	Yes	No
I feel overwhelmed by unfinished personal business.	Yes	No

Source: Used with permission from Overcoming Compassion Fatigue, Apr., 2000, Vol. 7, No. 4, *Family Practice Management.* Copyright © 2000 American Academy of Family Physicians. All rights reserved.

LEADER CREDIBILITY

ESSENTIAL QUESTION: How can you ensure that you are credible in the eyes of the school community?

YOUR GOAL: The people in the school community trust me, see me as competent and dynamic, and feel a sense of closeness to me.

When students believe that they can learn from their teachers, they are much more likely to do so. In the research world, this is known as teacher credibility. And the effect size is 1.09— Super powerful. But the four aspects of teacher credibility also apply to leaders. And leader credibility impacts the overall climate of the school.

So, what are the components of credibility and how can leaders ensure that they are credible with members of the school community? There are four components, which we will explore now.

Trust. Teachers, staff, and community members need to know that their leaders really care about them as individuals and have their best interests at heart. Members of the school community also want to know that their leaders are true to their word and are reliable. A few points about trust:

1. If you make a promise, work to keep it (or explain why you could not).

2. Tell staff members the truth about their performance (they know when their work is below standard and wonder why you are telling them otherwise).

3. Don't spend all of your time trying to catch staff members in the wrong (and yet be honest about the impact that their behavior has on you as an individual).

4. Examine any negative feelings you have about specific individuals (they sense it and it compromises the trust within the virtual classroom).

As Covey (2008) noted in *The Speed of Trust*, when it exists, things go faster. These more generic recommendations will continue to serve us well in a distance learning format. But there are additional considerations. In fact, Hoy and Tschannen-Moran identified five elements for trust to be developed and maintained, including (as defined by von Frank, 2010):

- **Benevolence:** *Confidence that one's well-being or something one cares about will be protected by the trusted party . . . the assurance that others will not exploit one's vulnerability or take advantage even when the opportunity is available.*

- **Honesty:** *The trusted person's character, integrity, and authenticity . . . acceptance of responsibility for one's actions and not distorting the truth in order to shift blame to another.*

- **Openness:** *The extent to which relevant information is shared . . . openness signals reciprocal trust.*

- **Reliability:** *Consistency of behavior and knowing what to expect from others . . . a sense of confidence that one's needs will be met in positive ways.*

- **Competency:** *The ability to perform as expected and according to standards appropriate to the task at hand* (p. 2).

Competence. In addition to trust, people want to know that their leaders know their stuff. They expect an appropriate level of expertise and accuracy from their leaders. When interacting with staff and community members,

1. Make sure you know the information well and be honest when a question arises that you are not sure about (this requires planning in advance).

2. Present yourself as confident. Of course, there are things we do not yet know, but people want to know that their leaders have made sound decisions that they stand by until better information is available.

3. Challenge ideas but not individuals. Your competence is compromised when people feel attacked.

4. Consider your nonverbal behaviors that communicate competence, such as the position of your hands when you talk with others or the facial expressions you make (people notice defensive positions, and nonverbal indications that they are not valued when they speak).

Dynamism. This dimension of credibility focuses on the passion you bring to your position. It is really about your ability to communicate enthusiasm. To improve dynamism,

1. *Rekindle the passion you have for leading.* Focus on the aspects that got you excited when you made the decision to leave the classroom. Remember why you wanted to be a leader.

2. *Collect success stories and share them.* Speak about successes with passion. Show your emotions. You are allowed to be happy, excited, and proud of the accomplishments of your team, and remember to attribute the success to their efforts.

3. *Work on your charisma.* When you present information, people are watching you as much as they are focused on the content. Your presentation slides can destroy your charisma, as can your tone of voice. Project your voice and pay attention to the inflections, pauses, and emphases. And update those presentation slides. If you need help, *Presentation Zen* (Reynolds, 2008) is a good source.

Immediacy. This final construct of credibility focuses on accessibility and relatability as perceived by others. The concept of immediacy was introduced by social psychologist Albert Mehrabian (1971) who noted that "people are drawn toward persons and things they like, evaluate highly, and prefer; and they avoid or move away from things they dislike, evaluate negatively, or do not prefer" (p. 1). Consider the following examples of general things you can do to ensure that people feel close to you:

- Gesture when talking.
- Look at people and smile while talking.
- Call people by name.
- Use *we* and *us* to refer to the team.
- Invite people to provide feedback.
- Use vocal variety (pauses, inflections, stress, emphasis) when talking to the class.

In addition, immediacy can be maintained from a distance by having many touchpoints with staff members. You'll note that there are sections focused on being visible and holding advisories. If there ever was a time for virtual office hours, distance learning is that time. People want to feel connected and assured that they are doing the right thing. Your credibility will impact the overall climate of the school and the learning your students do.

MAKE IT ACTIONABLE

How credible are you with members of the school community? How can you maintain and expand your credibility while working from a distance? Let's take a look at the tool on the next page and think about ways to ensure leader credibility.

COMPONENT OF CREDIBILITY	WAYS TO MAINTAIN AND IMPROVE FROM A DISTANCE (*ADD TO THE LIST WE HAVE STARTED*)
Trust	• Take notes when you make a promise and work to follow through. • Be honest, and kind, with feedback. • Demonstrate that you care about the well-being of others. • • • • •
Competence	• Plan informational sessions in advance so that you are confident. • Answer questions and acknowledge when you do not know something (and then find out and report back). • Check your confidence. Are you projecting confidence? • • • • •
Dynamism	• Refocus on your passion. Why did you become a leader? • Collect success stories and share them. • Review your presentation slides. • • • • •
Immediacy	• Be visible in a variety of places. • Video some interactions and analyze your nonverbal behaviors. • Seek feedback from others. • • • •

Given the importance of trust in school climate and leader credibility, we encourage you to offer staff members an opportunity to provide anonymous feedback about trust. The following tool (Figure 1.2) allows you to assess the trust teachers have for the principal, their colleagues, and the students and their families. The scoring key includes

Faculty Trust in the Principal—Items 1, 4*, 7, 9, 11*, 15, 18, 23*

Faculty Trust in Colleagues—Items 2, 5, 8*, 12, 13, 16, 19, 21

Faculty Trust in the Clients—Items 3, 6, 10, 14, 17, 20, 22, 24, 25, 26*

*Items are reversed scored, that is, [1 = 6, 2 = 5, 3 = 4, 4 = 3, 5 = 2, 6 = 1]

More information about scoring and determining where you stand in relation to other schools can be found at https://www.waynekhoy.com/faculty-trust/. Remember, these tools were developed in physical school, so take the findings with a bit of caution. Having said that, we think it's worth the effort to monitor trust as we work from a distance.

Figure 1.2 Omnibus T-Scale

Directions: Please indicate your level of agreement with each of the following statements about your school from **strongly disagree** to **strongly agree**. Your answers are confidential.

	Strongly Disagree	Disagree	Somewhat Disagree	Somewhat Agree	Agree	Strongly Agree
1. Teachers in this school trust the principal.	1	2	3	4	5	6
2. Teachers in this school trust each other.	1	2	3	4	5	6
3. Teachers in this school trust their students.	1	2	3	4	5	6
4. The teachers in this school are suspicious of most of the principal's actions.	1	2	3	4	5	6
5. Teachers in this school typically look out for each other.	1	2	3	4	5	6
6. Teachers in this school trust the parents.	1	2	3	4	5	6
7. The teachers in this school have faith in the integrity of the principal.	1	2	3	4	5	6
8. Teachers in this school are suspicious of each other.	1	2	3	4	5	6
9. The principal in this school typically acts in the best interests of teachers.	1	2	3	4	5	6
10. Students in this school care about each other.	1	2	3	4	5	6
11. The principal of this school does not show concern for the teachers.	1	2	3	4	5	6
12. Even in difficult situations, teachers in this school can depend on each other.	1	2	3	4	5	6
13. Teachers in this school do their jobs well.	1	2	3	4	5	6
14. Parents in this school are reliable in their commitments.	1	2	3	4	5	6
15. Teachers in this school can rely on the principal.	1	2	3	4	5	6
16. Teachers in this school have faith in the integrity of their colleagues.	1	2	3	4	5	6
17. Students in this school can be counted on to do their work.	1	2	3	4	5	6
18. The principal in this school is competent in doing his or her job.	1	2	3	4	5	6
19. The teachers in this school are open with each other.	1	2	3	4	5	6
20. Teachers can count on parental support.	1	2	3	4	5	6
21. When teachers in this school tell you something, you can believe it.	1	2	3	4	5	6
22. Teachers here believe students are competent learners.	1	2	3	4	5	6
23. The principal doesn't tell teachers what is really going on.	1	2	3	4	5	6
24. Teachers think that most of the parents do a good job.	1	2	3	4	5	6
25. Teachers can believe what parents tell them.	1	2	3	4	5	6
26. Students here are secretive.	1	2	3	4	5	6

Source: Copyright © Hoy and Tschannen-Moran (2003).

online resources 🔖 Available for download at **resources.corwin.com/DLPlaybook-leaders**

ESSENTIAL QUESTION: How can I distribute leadership responsibilities to maximize impact?

YOUR GOAL: Mobilize the team to ensure all students learn.

You are not alone. Perhaps you don't have assistant principals or coordinators, but you do have others who are willing to help. The instructional leadership team could be your administrative team, or it could be your grade-level or department representatives. If you are in the district office, it might be the cabinet or a team of teachers on special assignment. In distance learning, we can forget the value of involving others in the decision-making process. In spring 2020, too many leaders ended up unintentionally isolating themselves, in part because they thought they were being helpful to others who had new responsibilities and the stress from working at home. Others realized the power of a collective effort and increased their adoption of distributed leadership.

The idea of distributed leadership has been around for some time (e.g., Leithwood, Mascall, & Strauss, 2009). It's also fairly misunderstood. It's not assigning people your work and then abdicating responsibility. In fact, distributed leadership is not about delegating. Instead, it's about getting work done in a more efficient way while also increasing the leadership capacity within the organization. As Midles and Nichols (2020) noted, "Distributed leadership is a counternarrative to traditional, isolated, expertise-focused leadership models." As Solly (2018) described it, distributed leadership requires three inter-connected parts:

> DISTRIBUTED LEADERSHIP IS ABOUT GETTING WORK DONE IN A MORE EFFICIENT WAY WHILE ALSO INCREASING THE LEADERSHIP CAPACITY WITHIN THE ORGANIZATION.

- **Autonomy:** Members of a distributed leadership team need to be given the autonomy to make decisions in their areas of responsibilities. For distributed leadership to work, members of the team cannot continually seek permission to make decisions. That undermines their authority and sends a message to the person waiting for the decision that they should have "gone to the top" in the first place. As they make appropriate decisions, members of leadership teams can earn more autonomy.

- **Accountability:** As individuals make more decisions within their areas of responsibility, they need to be held accountable for those decisions. Some decisions might not have been the best, and the person who made that decision needs to learn from it. And sometimes, decisions have to be reversed. But learning from those situations is important and saves time in the long run as teams become more efficient.

- **Capacity:** Members of distributed leadership teams need to develop the skills necessary to complete their responsibilities. Providing people with the tools they need is an ongoing process. As they earn more autonomy and have increased accountability, new learning is likely necessary.

But why is this important in distance learning? The leaders who we learned from had to lean on their teams to be effective. They could not be in every video conference. They could not answer every question that arose. And they could not support the learning of others as distance learning instruction improved. The schools that maintained or improved their distributed leadership had less stressed leaders and a greater impact on students and teachers. As the saying goes, no person is an island. Leadership can be a lonely job. Why make it more lonely than it needs to be? Some leaders delegated assemblies and others delegated attendance monitoring. Still others created teams to design professional learning experiences and others to manage supply pick-up days.

Trust your team. Empower them. Add responsibilities and provide the support so that they can make good decisions. Develop feedback loops so that you can provide monitoring and support as the team becomes increasingly sophisticated in solving problems and innovating. DeFlaminis, Abdul-Jabbar, and Yoak (2016) describe several levels of leadership. Level 5, distributed leadership, includes the definition and roles shown in Figure 1.3.

Figure 1.3 Level 5: Distributed Leadership

The leader is no longer central to the team and greater interdependence develops and exists between the team members and the leader. The leader has delegated some responsibilities and decisions and the team's authority has increased.

The Leader	Team Members
• Has shifted from sole doer to supporter, coach, and facilitator in distributed areas.	• Assume distributed duties/areas with little assistance from the leader.
• Works with team to expand authority to higher level responsibilities.	• Work closely with school staffs and, in many cases, other team members. Some form their own networks.
• Coordinates the team efforts.	• Assume distributed responsibilities formerly held by the leader and have decision-making authority in those areas.
• Allows others to direct organization members in influencing distributed areas of the core work.	• Direct organization members in influencing distributed areas of the core work.

Source: Copyright © 2016. From *Distributed Leadership* by John A. DeFlamnis, Mustfa Abdul-Jabbar, and Eric Yoak. Reproduced by permission of Taylor and Francis Group, LLC, a division of Informa plc. This permission does not cover any third party copyrighted work which may appear in the material requested. User is responsible for obtaining permission for such material separately from this grant.

MAKE IT ACTIONABLE

Do you have a plan in place to mobilize your instructional leadership team? How is it working for you? For distributed leadership to work, individuals must understand their major leadership functions. Clarity in responsibilities is critical and worth the time investment.

Major Leadership Functions

Name: _____   Leadership Function: _____

Expectations	Reflective Questions	Your Responses
It becomes a part of your identity and accountability to lead, not just manage.	What does it mean to have responsibility for this major leadership function?	
Annual Goal	How will it be different in one year?	
30-Day Plan	Describe what it will look like when it is really going well. Paint the picture.	
60-Day Plan	Describe what it will look like when it is really going well. Paint the picture.	
90-Day Plan	Describe what it will look like when it is really going well. Paint the picture.	

Your Data Story for This Leadership Function

Hard and Soft Data	Baseline and Benchmarks

Your Communication Plan for This Leadership Function

Monthly Action Agenda Communication	What are its implications for the following?
	• Leadership team • Staffing support • Budget • Other administrative support • Professional learning
Monthly Reports	• Stakeholder updates • Accountability reports

online resources ☞ Available for download at **resources.corwin.com/DLPlaybook-leaders**

STAKEHOLDER ADVISORY GROUPS

The governance of the school doesn't stop because distance learning is in place. Schools have always had a host of committees to explore an ongoing topic. These committees often include those who advise on issues related to English learners and students with disabilities, as just two examples. In addition, schools employ student governance to advise on decisions about student life. Other internal committees may include those charged with instruction and curriculum, and for classified and clerical staff.

Indeed, the effectiveness of schools is associated with stakeholder voice. The Consortium for Chicago Schools Research (CCSR) examined what characteristics distinguish thriving schools from those that don't. The mediators, it turns out, were not urbanicity, demographics, socioeconomic status, or the number of languages spoken. Over a period of seven years, the CCSR examined what happened at 100 Chicago Public Schools that had made substantial gains in reading scores, grades, attendance, and family satisfaction, all while reducing educator turnover. These qualitative and quantitative data were compared to 100 CPS schools that had stagnated results (Bryk, Sebring, Allensworth, Luppescu, & Easton, 2010). What characteristics separated these schools, all of which were in the same district?

> **ESSENTIAL QUESTION:** How can I gain a multidimensional view of stakeholder experiences in distance learning?
>
> **YOUR GOAL:** Increase staff, student, and family voice about distance learning to respond to challenges and take successes to scale.

- *A student-centered learning climate* that is safe, orderly, and attuned to its learners.
- *The professional capacity of staff* to embrace innovation, commit to the well-being of the school, and assert a collective responsibility for every student in the school (not just on their own rosters.)
- *Ties to families and communities* with high levels of teacher–parent trust, and parent involvement in school decision making.
- *School leadership* that values program coherence, instructional leadership, and teacher influence.

Key to accomplishing these outcomes is to ensure that stakeholders are empowered to make decisions and voice concerns. In a time when distance learning has become the "next normal," school leaders need to gather the insights of staff, students, and families to strengthen learning experiences. Greater stakeholder engagement that is meaningful is crucial in a time of change for schools.

MAKE IT ACTIONABLE

Leading at a distance means that it is more challenging to get the feedback you need to monitor progress toward school goals. Form advisory groups of three to eight people and meet with them at least monthly to gauge how the school's efforts are being received by constituents. These meetings can range from thirty to sixty minutes in length and are improved with an agenda that focuses inquiry on a particular topic. In creating a safe virtual space for advisory meetings, you are modeling respect and high expectations for the school community. These actions make you better prepared to be responsive to the diverse needs of students, staff, and families. The distance learning equity questions posed are inspired by Education Trust (2020), who remind us that we are all equity advocates.

Sample Topics to Explore With Advisory Groups	
Teachers	• *Professional Learning:* How can professional learning be improved to align with current needs? • *Successes and Growth:* What is working for you currently, and where should we focus efforts for improvement? • *Innovation:* What have you encountered recently that you believe might strengthen our distance learning program? • *Equity:* Are we meeting the needs of students with varying levels of access to the internet and technology?
Students	• *Student Learning Experience:* What are your experiences this month in distance learning? • *Student Voice:* How do we make our school a more welcoming place for students during distance learning? • *Improving Our School:* What do you see other students struggling with? How can we be better for them? • *Equity:* Do you know your academic progress in distance learning? What could we do to improve your knowledge of your progress?
Clerical Staff	• *Improving Our Customers' Experience:* How might we improve our interface with students? Colleagues? Families? • *Successes and Growth:* What is working for you currently, and where should we focus efforts for improvement? • *Innovation:* What have you encountered recently that you believe might improve your work experience? • *Equity:* What inequities are you encountering as you work with colleagues, students, and families?
Families	• *Family Voice:* How do we make school a more welcoming place for families during distance learning? • *Community Needs and Resources:* What are unmet needs in our community? What community resources should we be leveraging? • *Family Partnerships:* What is working for you in terms of communication? What should there be more or less of? How can the school be a better partner for you and other families? • *Equity:* How do we support the social and emotional well-being of parents and caregivers?

VIRTUAL VISIBILITY

School leaders shape the climate in part by maintaining a high degree of visibility for all stakeholders. Those with more positive school climates prioritize being a visible presence, while those with a more negative climate often prioritize paperwork (Fiore, 2000). In a face-to-face environment, this might include actions such as greeting students and families as they arrive and depart the building, being in the hallways during passing periods and at lunch, and spending time in classrooms. However, during distance learning many of these possibilities are limited or nonexistent.

The research on distance learning includes an intriguing element we rarely consider in a brick-and-mortar school: visibility in virtual environments. Virtual visibility is your social, emotional, and cognitive presence in the online life of the school (Garrison, Anderson, & Archer, 2000). It connects with the immediacy we noted in the section on teacher clarity but immediacy is the sense of closeness you feel when you are present. This is a reminder to be present.

ESSENTIAL QUESTION: How can I remain visible and accessible to students, staff, and families when our school is in distance learning?

YOUR GOAL: Extend your visibility by enacting strategies to boost your social, emotional, and cognitive presence.

Certainly, many young people are attuned to this. After all, some social media influencers have a staggering number of followers. Why don't you take a page or two from their playbook to be an influencer in your own school? According to Influencer Marketing Hub, an agency dedicated to supporting social media influencers, there are seven steps to becoming one. We've used those as inspiration to link these to school leadership:

1. **Select your niche.** That's a pretty straightforward one—it's your school organization!

2. **Optimize your social media profiles.** Make sure your school is represented across major platforms, including Twitter, Instagram, and Facebook. In addition, use a two-way communication system (e.g., Remind, or a portal in your school's learning management system.)

3. **Understand your audience.** Develop plans that target students, staff, and families, as each of these audiences has unique needs.

4. **Create and post relevant content.** Short video messages and Instagram Stories threads make you a regular presence.

5. **Be regular and consistent.** It's easy to forget or to let a few days go by because you're doing so many other things. Scheduling platforms allow you to create content in batches and deploy it automatically in the future.

6. **Engage with your audience.** Whatever platform you are posting on, be sure to check it regularly so you can answer questions and acknowledge comments.

7. **Let brands know you're open to collaborations.** The "brands" in this case are your stakeholders. One of the best ways to signal your willingness to collaborate is to profile the collaboration you're already doing with advisory groups, committees, and teams.

MAKE IT ACTIONABLE

Send a daily welcome message. Morning announcements are ubiquitous in schools. Record and deploy announcements each day so that teachers can use them in their virtual sessions. Lead the Pledge of Allegiance or have a different student each day do it virtually as part of your announcements. Play the school song. Demonstrate your personality, whether it is a mindful minute, a joke of the day, or a favorite quote.

Be a regular presence in live virtual sessions. Students and teachers were accustomed to seeing school leaders visiting their classrooms. That's even more important in distance learning. Your presence is encouraging for children and adults, as it reminds them that schooling is not a solitary experience, but rather a communal one.

Conduct emotional check-ins with staff. You counted on informally checking in with staff in the hallways and other public spaces throughout the day in a brick-and-mortar setting. Set aside time in your calendar to meet individually with staff members on a rotating basis. A few short conversations a day by each member of your administrative team means that you will have met individually with each adult in a matter of weeks. When you're done, start again.

Send messages to students and families. Use your school's mobile messaging service or autodialer to send messages to families about current events at the school. Pose a question that families can discuss with their children (e.g., "What makes you unique?" or "What makes you feel better when you're upset?") or give some daily trivia about the date in history. These short reminders reinforce the importance of your school community, even at a distance.

Hold office hours for families. Families appreciate being able to have impromptu conversations, and that can continue virtually. As part of the weekly announcements you send to families, let them know how they can participate in office hours you host.

THE FEEL OF SCHOOL

ESSENTIAL QUESTION: How does the school "feel" to students and staff?

YOUR GOAL: Create a sense of belonging and ownership of school from a distance.

Schools have a feel to them. It's noticeable from the first moments when you enter the building. Some schools are filled with spirit. Others are a bit sad. Some schools have art along the walls and proudly display student accomplishments. And schools have different feels. In part, it's the pride students and staff have for their school. It's manifest in the building, but it's more than that, as we have learned from distance learning.

Leaders who maintain the feel of their school during distance learning have more students log-in to distance learning more frequently. And students in those schools talked about being part of something bigger. They said things like "My school has an assembly every Monday" or "We got shirts from the school so that we could wear them if we wanted on spirit days." In these cases, students felt like they belonged. They were connected to others who shared the same experience.

We recognize that maintaining the feel of school can be difficult from a distance. It's hard to feel part of something when you aren't there. But there are things that leaders can do to create a sense of belonging. For example, virtual backgrounds can be branded with school colors, names, and mascots. You can still have spirit days. You can have assemblies and special events. You can still celebrate accomplishments and achievements.

We were reminded by one administrator that we still needed to "live our values." Some time ago, we identified five pillars that contributed to a culture of achievement (Fisher, Frey, & Pumpian, 2012). Our role now is to translate these pillars into a distance learning environment:

- **Welcome**: Imagine if all staff members in your school considered it their job to make every student, parent, and visitor feel noticed, welcomed, and valued.

- **Do no harm**: Your school rules should be tools for teaching students to become the moral and ethical citizens you expect them to be.

- **Choice words**: When the language students hear helps them tell a story about themselves that is one of possibility and potential, students perform in ways that are consistent with that belief.

- **It's never too late to learn**: Can you push students to go beyond the minimum needed to get by, to discover what they are capable of achieving?

- **Best school in the universe**: Is your school the best place to teach and learn? The best place to work?

The question is, how do you deliver on these values, or the ones you hold dear, from a distance? Our recommendation is that you talk with your advisory groups and brainstorm a number of possibilities to establish, maintain, and grow the feel of the school. For example, you may want to consider how the various pages of the learning management system convey welcoming. You may also want to consider the ways that teachers address problematic behavior during synchronous learning so that students learn from the mistakes that they make.

MAKE IT ACTIONABLE

One of the actions you can take is to periodically survey people about the experiences that they are having with the school. You might randomly select 10 percent of the families and send them a survey. Or the students. Or the teachers and staff. As an example, use the survey in Figure 1.4 to seek feedback about the efforts to support family members. You can use parts of it or the whole thing. Of course, you'd want to provide this in the languages spoken by the families in your school.

Figure 1.4 Family Survey

We would like to know your opinions on how well our school is meeting your family's and child(ren)'s needs and how you feel about your satisfaction with the school experience.

- There are no right or wrong answers.
- We are interested only in your opinions.
- Your answers will be kept private. Your answers will be combined with those of other parents in a report of the survey findings.
- Your input is very important. Findings of the survey will be summarized and used to improve the school's efforts in strengthening the partnership between parents and the school.

What is/are your child(ren)'s grade level(s)? (circle all that apply)

K   1   2   3   4   5   6   7   8   9   10   11   12

Were any of these children enrolled at our school last year?   ☐ Yes   ☐ No

When you contact the school,	All of the Time	Most of the Time	Some of the Time	None of the Time
Is the office staff friendly and helpful?				
Are the teachers easy to talk to?				
Are the administrators easy to talk to?				
Do you feel welcomed?				

What is/are the best way(s) to communicate with you and/or your family? (choose all that apply)

☐ School memos (emails, website, letters, etc.)

☐ Children's teachers

☐ Counselor

☐ Direct contact (phone call, school/home visit, meeting)

☐ Other—please specify: _____

What else would you like to tell us about communication at our school?

_____

_____

_____

_____

_____

_____

Last school year, were you contacted by someone from the school regarding any of the following? (choose all that apply)

☐ Your child's academic success

☐ Your child's academic struggles

☐ Your child's positive social behavior

☐ Your child's negative social behavior

☐ Your child's achievements (music, volunteerism, etc.)

☐ No reason, just to make contact (say hello, introduce self, etc.)

☐ Other—please specify: _____

What else would you like to tell us about contact regarding your child's successes and difficulties?

_____

_____

_____

_____

_____

How much do you agree or disagree with the following statements?	Strongly Agree	Agree	Disagree	Strongly Disagree
The school has high expectations for my child.				
The school clearly communicates those expectations to me and my child(ren).				
My child is learning what they need to know to be successful after graduating.				
My child receives assistance when they are having difficulty academically or socially.				
The curriculum and activities keep my child interested and motivated.				
My child is happy at school.				

What activities would you like to see added to our distance learning? Why?

_____

_____

_____

_____

_____

(Continued)

(Continued)

What activities would you like us to continue from our physical classrooms? Why?

_____

_____

_____

_____

_____

What activities would you like us to delete? Why?

_____

_____

_____

_____

_____

What activities would you like us to change? Why?

_____

_____

_____

_____

_____

What else would you like to tell us about learning at our school?

_____

_____

_____

_____

_____

**Thank you for taking the time to complete this survey. We can't be
the Best School in the Universe without families like yours.**

Source: Republished with permission of the Association for Supervision & Curriculum Development, from *How to create a culture of achievement in your school and classroom*, Fisher, D., Frey, N., & Pumpian, I. (2012); permission conveyed through Copyright Clearance Center, Inc.

online resources ⟋ Available for download at **resources.corwin.com/DLPlaybook-leaders**

The climate of the school is still important, even as learners learn and teachers teach from a distance. Monitoring and managing the experience that people have with the organization is an important role that the leader has. It's not the only role, but it's useful to maintain the uniqueness of your school. People want to feel part of something special and know that their efforts matter. You can help ensure that they have that feeling.

2 PROFESSIONAL LEARNING AT A DISTANCE

If there ever was a time to invest in the learning of adults, it's now. And the learning needed is more than technology. Teachers need support to develop engaging lessons and help determining their impact. They need to be supported to collaborate with their colleagues to learn from one another. And they need to see you, their leader, as a learner. But learning is not limited to teachers. As the leader, you have the opportunity to impact the entire support system for the students in your school, which includes people in the home who can play a role in learning.

In this section:

- [ ] LEARNING BELIEFS AT A DISTANCE
- [ ] COLLABORATIVE INQUIRY CYCLES
- [ ] INPUT TRAINING
- [ ] SAFE PRACTICE
- [ ] VIRTUAL LEARNING WALKS

- [ ] MICROTEACHING IN DISTANCE LEARNING
- [ ] PERSONALIZED PROFESSIONAL LEARNING
- [ ] SOCIAL PRESENCE
- [ ] PARENT EDUCATION AND SUPPORT

WE CAN'T HOPE FOR CHANGE IF WE ARE NOT PRESENT. WE CAN'T HOPE FOR CHANGE IF WE DON'T PROVIDE TIME FOR HONEST FEEDBACK AND TRUE REFLECTION BASED ON WHAT WE OBSERVE.

Some families of budding athletes hire a private coach to work on a set of technical skills to improve their student's athletic performance. The coach tells the young athletes what to do and then sends them to their games. Does the private coach ever show up to the game? If the answer is "No," how would that coach teach what needs to change? They would have no idea and soon word would get around to the other parents that the private coach wasn't very effective.

School leaders run professional development all the time and want teachers to improve. They expect to see change, but some rarely if ever show up to the class. We can't hope for change if we are not present. We can't hope for change if we don't provide time for honest feedback and true reflection based on what we observe.

The six principles of adult learning theory should always inform professional learning. Knowles (1970) called it _andragogy_. Essentially, it is the art and science of helping adults learn and includes the following:

1. Adults are self-directed and internally motivated.

2. Adults bring knowledge and experiences to their learning.

3. Adults are goal oriented.

4. Adults are relevancy oriented.

5. Adults are practical.

6. Adults need to feel respected.

The most effective professional learning is therefore relevant and applicable while honoring their knowledge and experiences. The learning should always be accompanied by opportunities to set goals, self-assess, and self-direct their own learning.

The professional learning needs of teachers continues even at a distance. The good news is that there is no need to gather in the multipurpose room for a one-size-fits-all session that may be of limited benefit to some teachers due to existing expertise or lack of relevance. But if we fail to be present in virtual classrooms, and we don't demonstrate the kind of shoulder-to-shoulder effort that results in collective learning, professional learning slows to a crawl. And this is precisely the time when we can't afford for that to occur. As distance learning school leaders, we can and should be amplifying the emerging promising practices of teachers to ensure that they don't remain as silos of excellence.

Noting that "the old playbook for professional learning likely won't suffice" in the shift to distance learning (Rivero, 2020, p. 26), Student Achievement Partners, a nonprofit organization dedicated to supporting school leaders and teachers in developing free standards-aligned resources, outlined priorities for professional learning (Student Achievement Partners [SAP], 2020):

1. **Professional learning should be content focused.** Build teachers' content and pedagogical knowledge for teaching and assessing at a distance.

2. **Professional learning should be teacher and student centered.** Promote collective responsibility for student learning and cultivate a culture in which adults learn from one another.

3. **Professional learning should be instructionally relevant and actionable.** Professional learning should be anchored in the distance learning priorities of teachers as it relates to instruction, curriculum, and assessment. These are achieved by cycles of inquiry that include classroom practice, observations, and feedback. Cycles of professional learning are linked to evidence of student learning.

A reenergized professional learning plan for distance learning enacts what we have known all along: Personalize the learning to meet the needs of individual teachers and connect teachers so they can learn together. There are times when whole-staff learning is still warranted, but it is only the tip of the iceberg. Couple this with other practices that include grade level micro-events, personalized learning, and inquiry cycles.

Reserve large-group professional learning sessions for initial acquisition of knowledge. Schoolwide sessions are useful to establish foundational knowledge about a topic or concept. For example, an introduction to distance learning practices, a new assessment system, or new curricular materials might warrant an initial virtual session.

Follow up with grade- or department-specific microevents. Get specific feedback from teachers and process learning together with short live session meetings led by a school leader or instructional coach. Ask them how they are contextualizing the information and what they need next to continue their learning.

Have each teacher build a personalized learning plan. There is a wealth of online learning opportunities from formal courses to virtual EdCamps to specialized social media groups. Ask each teacher to propose a plan for their own learning that taps into their interests, strengths, and growth areas.

Leverage the collective power of professional learning communities. The school as a whole is a professional learning community, with smaller specialized groups operating together on a common challenge. Build inquiry cycles into the professional learning community process.

Round out learning with professional learning check-ins. These might be done by school learners, instructional coaches, teacher–leaders, or any combination. Check in with teachers once per quarter to find out about their progress on their personalized learning plan.

Before you move into this section of the playbook, take a few minutes to self-assess the current conditions of professional learning at a distance.

DRAWING ON MY EXPERTISE

How is virtual professional learning continuing at your school? Use the traffic light scale to reflect on current practices. To what extent is each of these statements true?

	1. I survey teachers to learn about their professional needs.
	2. Professional learning processes include knowledge acquisition, coaching, and follow-up.
	3. I observe in virtual classrooms to understand the impact of professional learning.
	4. I actively participate in coaching and feedback that is growth producing.
	5. The work of PLCs is directly tied to the professional learning at the school.
	6. Teachers learn with and from one another.
	7. I give parents support as partners in learning.

LEARNING BELIEFS AT A DISTANCE

ESSENTIAL QUESTION: Do the learning beliefs of teachers enhance or inhibit distance learning?

YOUR GOAL: Identify teachers' core beliefs about learning in order to develop professional learning experiences.

Teachers' beliefs shape the way they make decisions about learning, instruction, and assessment. These beliefs are influenced by their preparation, as well as their personal experiences. For example, some teachers have a linear orientation and thus believe that skills must be taught in a specific order, while others prefer a holistic approach. In a distance learning setting, assumptions about teaching and learning are being challenged. For example, how are long-standing practices in your school about grading, differentiation, and even discipline being reinterpreted in a virtual environment?

A needs assessment in advance of planning professional learning is always wise. It is far more difficult for an instructional leadership team (ILT) to make thoughtful decisions about the direction for the year in the absence of input from the faculty. However, we also believe that simply presenting a laundry list of possible topics isn't useful either. There can be a tendency to check off items one already knows quite a bit about, rather than considering new learnings.

MAKE IT ACTIONABLE

An exploration of learning beliefs can give you and the ILT insight into attitudes and beliefs of the faculty such that problems can be addressed more directly. In addition, the results can become a starting point for identifying a common challenge for the professional learning inquiry cycle (see the next module). The survey itself should be anonymous, of course, with clear assurances about confidentiality. You might use the one in Figure 2.1 or develop one of your own.

Figure 2.1   Learning Beliefs Survey

Please respond to the following statements according to the scale below:

1 = Strongly Agree

2 = Somewhat Agree

3 = Somewhat Disagree

4 = Strongly Disagree

_____ 1. I feel that our educational system is working.

_____ 2. I feel that I have the training to implement high quality instruction successfully.

_____ 3. I feel that I cover less of the curriculum because of the focus on acceleration.

_____ 4. I feel that I have the time to implement quality instruction effectively.

_____ 5. I feel that grades are fixed and should not be changed once assigned.

_____ 6. I feel that it is difficult to modify instruction and my teaching style to meet the needs of all of my students.

_____ 7. I feel that allowing students multiple opportunities to demonstrate mastery is fair.

_____ 8. I feel that having other adults in my classroom is a problem.

_____ 9. I feel that the behaviors of some students distract the rest of a class and take away from time spent teaching.

_____ 10. I feel that students take advantage of grading systems designed to be flexible.

Please complete this thought:

Learning is best accomplished when _____

_____

_____

_____

online resources   Available for download at **resources.corwin.com/DLPlaybook-leaders**

COLLABORATIVE INQUIRY CYCLES

ESSENTIAL QUESTION: How can professional learning occur in a distance learning environment?

YOUR GOAL: Frame professional learning using systematic phases that promote adult learning in virtual environments.

Professional learning is vital in distance learning as school teams refine their synchronous and asynchronous instruction. Learning together with and from colleagues, rather than in isolation, speeds the learning of the organization. A collaborative inquiry cycle draws on the research about goal attainment, trust, and knowledge building, as well as the work of others (DeWitt, 2019; Donohoo, 2013; Knight, 2007). These phases contribute to the collective efficacy of the teams as they learn together. As a school community, this process links collective efficacy to what Hoy and Tschannen call "the normative and behavioral environment of the school" (as defined by von Frank, 2010). The components of this model are not strictly linear. Rather, they are essential habits for moving adult learning forward while building the relational strengths among professional colleagues to take on the work. We have used the inquiry of a middle school mathematics team to illustrate a ten-week example of a collaborative inquiry cycle in Figure 2.2.

Activate your instructional leadership team. Your ILT sets the direction for department or grade-level learning and provides the initial input training that builds a foundation of knowledge. In the case of the middle school, the ILT identified that bringing rigor into the distance learning program at the school was an essential next step. "We recognized that our first order of business was to get a cohesive distance learning program in place," said principal Tisha Washington. "Now we're turning our attention to improving the rigor as students and teachers have adjusted."

Identify the common challenge. At the risk of stating the obvious, teams perform better when there is a shared goal. Tasks can then be focused on steady progress toward the goal, rather than activities that fill time but do not yield results. An agreed-upon common challenge is one that is publicly acknowledged, is observable and actionable, and mobilizes teachers to take action (Fisher, Frey, Almarode, Flories, & Nagel, 2020a, 2020b). During a virtual PLC meeting, the math team decided that their common challenge would be to foster more algebraic thinking in their seventh- and eighth-grade distance learning math classes.

Build knowledge and skills. New practices are typically introduced through initial professional learning sessions, shared or vicarious experiences, or professional readings. However, the habit of consulting sources to aid in ongoing practice is crucial. The math team utilized the district math coach to meet with them on a Zoom session, and they read several professional papers by mathematics researchers and practitioners.

Safe practice and collaborative planning. New professional learning should always include time for teachers to experiment as they take on a

Figure 2.2 Collaborative Inquiry Professional Learning Cycle

Cycle # / Date Span	ILT Meeting to Set Direction	Input Training	Safe Practice	Professional Reading	Opening Up Virtual Classroom Practice: Peer Observation and Reflection	Collaborative Planning	Monitor Measure Modify
	Planning and leading professional learning	2–3 meetings per PLC Professional learning for teachers on how to implement a practice	Teachers experiment with the new practice in a low-risk environment	At least 4 per PLC Teachers receive professional articles relevant to the practice being learned	Teachers observe each other and engage in structured reflection/feedback	2 virtual meetings per month: focus on PLC Teachers look at student work and data	ILT and staff engage in virtual learning walks to look for evidence of implementation
Week 1	School ILT 10/19			Professional reading "Algebra for All" 11/6 PLC+ mtg		11/6 PLC+ mtg (last year's data)	
Week 2		Meet with district math coach on Zoom 11/12		Professional reading on Equitable Algebra 11/12 PLC+ mtg			
Week 3		District Algebra for All virtual training 11/17				11/20 PLC+ mtg (student examples)	
Week 4	District Math ILT 11/30		11/30-12/4				
Week 5			12/7-12/11	Professional reading on student think-alouds 12/11 PLC+ mtg			

(Continued)

LEARNING

(Continued)

Cycle # Date Span	ILT Meeting to Set Direction — Planning and leading professional learning	Input Training — 2–3 meetings per PLC; Professional learning for teachers on how to implement a practice	Safe Practice — Teachers experiment with the new practice in a low-risk environment	Professional Reading — At least 4 per PLC; Teachers receive professional articles relevant to the practice being learned	Opening Up Virtual Classroom Practice: Peer Observation and Reflection — Teachers observe each other and engage in structured reflection/feedback	Collaborative Planning — 2 virtual meetings per month: focus on PLC; Teachers look at student work and data	Monitor Measure Modify — ILT and staff engage in virtual learning walks to look for evidence of implementation
Week 6	School ILT check-in 12/16				Ghost walks of LMS 12/17 PLC+ mtg	Analyze practice test results 12/17 PLC+ mtg	ILT faculty learning walk 12/14
Week 7					Capacity-building learning walks 1/4-1/8	Look at student exit tickets 1/8 PLC+ mtg	
Week 8			1/11-1/15	Professional reading on Algebra and English learners 1/15 PLC+ mtg			
Week 9					Micro-teaching 1/22 PLC+ mtg		
Week 10	School ILT 1/26				Capacity-building learning walks 1/25-1/29		ILT faculty learning walk 1/25

Source: Adapted from Chula Vista Elementary School District. Cycles of Professional Learning and this planning template developed by Targeted Leadership Consulting. www.targetedleadershipconsulting.net

new approach. With two weeks' worth of newly revised lessons in hand, the seventh- and eighth-grade math teachers first tried it out for themselves in their distance learning classes and shared their early impressions with their colleagues. Over time, they more fully incorporated these approaches into their instructional design.

Open up practice and collaborative planning. The entire team viewed each other's learning management systems to understand the asynchronous tasks students were completing. In addition, they had opportunities to sit in on each other's synchronous lessons. "We developed a schedule among ourselves so each person on our team got a chance to be a visitor and a host," said one member. Their collaborative planning continued, as members traded suggestions and piloted methods.

Monitor, measure, modify through collaborative planning. Throughout this unit, they met regularly to inform one another of what they were witnessing with their own students, adjusting as needed. Each made adjustments to tasks and instruction to improve their students' use of algebraic thinking.

Each professional learning community at the school posts their learning cycle in the school's professional learning folder. These publicly posted plans provide other teams with information about what their colleagues are doing, thus reinforcing the normative and behavioral environment of the school essential for building collective efficacy. There is something to be said for knowing that the colleagues you see more rarely when everyone is teaching at a distance are similarly engaged in their own professional learning. Knowing that all the proverbial oars are in the water and rowing in the same direction boosts morale and increases motivation. There are assurances to be derived from coordinated efforts like this. Members of high-performing rowing teams don't waste their energy turning around to make sure the person behind them is doing what is expected.

MAKE IT ACTIONABLE

A collaborative inquiry cycle of professional learning telegraphs two important messages to the teaching staff. The first is that we have moved beyond crisis teaching into the next normal. Schooling goes on for students and professional learning continues for adults. The second message is that the collaborative work of teams aligns with a belief that education improves though collective effort. With a staff that is working at a physical distance from one another, it requires intention to build community.

NOTE TO SELF

What collaborative inquiry practices do you already have in place? What do you plan to do next? Assess current professional learning at your site and prioritize your efforts.

	CURRENTLY DOING	PLANNING TO DO	TO CONSIDER
Professional learning is systematic and not limited to "one-shot" sessions on different topics.			
There is an ILT in place to guide the focus of professional learning.			
The work of professional learning communities is aligned to the professional learning of the school.			

INPUT TRAINING

ESSENTIAL QUESTION: What should I consider when planning a virtual professional development session?

YOUR GOAL: Make the most of professional learning sessions by aligning to goals and increasing interaction.

Virtual professional learning sessions require many of the same carefully considered steps needed in face-to-face learning. Wise practice begins with collaborating with your instructional leadership team to determine the focus of the inquiry cycle. These decisions set the direction for extended learning through professional learning communities, departments, or grade-level teams. Initial input training occurs early in the inquiry cycle and is used for knowledge building with teachers. A good foundation in the selected practice can provide teams with the springboard they need to launch their inquiry. However, delivering a professional learning event to your staff poses some considerations about the virtual platform and the logistics.

Have norms for your virtual sessions. Is there an expectation that cameras are on? What about professional attire? Is it OK for a participant to be working out on their treadmill or driving in the car? Build for success by proactively engaging in discussion with the staff about the norms for these sessions.

Use the platform that teachers are using in their classrooms. There are a variety of learning platforms that allow for live interactions, including Zoom, Google Meet, and Microsoft Teams. Each have their own advantages and drawbacks. When at all possible, use the same platform that teachers are using with their own students. It increases your credibility and offers opportunities to model features available in the platform.

Begin with an emotional check-in and set the purpose for the session. A sense of closeness is at a premium when everyone is learning at a distance. Set the tone by inviting people to take a deep breath and center themselves. You might ask a question (e.g., "What's the last thing a kid taught you how to do?") or invite a quick roundtable response (e.g., "What is one word that describes your morning so far?"). This allows the community to look around the virtual room and see one another right away. As you begin the session, be sure to include learning intentions and success criteria so that participants know the scope and expectations.

Promote frequent low-stakes interactions. Attention spans can be strained a bit in virtual learning, so provide interaction opportunities at regular intervals. The chat feature offers an easy way to pose questions and get immediate responses. Having said that, these questions should be readily answered using a minimal number of words. A second interaction function is polling. Many platforms offer a polling function as an add-on extension, but keep in mind that they must be programmed in advance.

Use breakout rooms for longer discussions. Breakout rooms provide a third kind of interaction. These should be reserved for questions that are substantive in nature, as the purpose is to foster longer discussions. Depending on your intentions, you might use these for random groupings or for team discussions. If they will be in teams, ask them at the beginning of the session to set their screen name so that it begins with the team designation (e.g., 8, Math, or Coach) so that you can quickly sort them into prearranged breakout rooms.

Solicit questions and feedback. Chunk the session into key points and provide time for people to respond. We recommend turning off the screen-sharing feature so that everyone can see each other. Pose a question that requires further thinking and ask participants to use the hand-raising feature so that everyone isn't talking at the same time. Call on teachers in order and invite them to turn their microphone on so they can comment verbally. These interactions can spark further discussion and foster ideas. Be sure to do so after breakout rooms as well so that you can get good ideas out to all participants.

LEARNING

Feedback about the content of the session is crucial for the instructional leadership team. Don't make the mistake of only asking about the length or comfort of the session. Follow-up coaching, team microevents, readings, and such can't happen without feedback from participants.

Designate someone on the team to manage logistics. This person is invaluable, as they can send tips in advance of the meeting to participants, especially if they are not yet comfortable with the technology. They can resend the link to the meeting the day of the event so that people aren't scrambling looking for it in last week's email. This person can also mute participants who accidentally turn their microphones on in the virtual main room and monitor the chat. If you use breakout rooms, this person can stay in the main room to handle any difficulty an individual might have while you join groups and listen for their ideas.

Plan for more frequent breaks. Anticipate that people will need short movement breaks and comfort breaks more often than in a face-to-face professional learning event. It is better to cover a little less content in order to increase attention.

Build in time for reflection. Virtual professional learning sessions can take on the feel of trying to drink water out of a fire hose—too much information. Make sure there are planned times for people to reflect and make notes for themselves at regular intervals. Just as with students, they need time to process, monitor their own understanding, and formulate questions.

MAKE IT ACTIONABLE

Planning a virtual professional learning session has much in common with principles of adult learning: make it relevant, practical, and actionable and align it to goals. Thoughtful planning of a virtual learning session conveys the respect you have for them as people and as professionals.

NOTE TO SELF

Use the checklist to ensure that your next virtual professional learning session is successful.

	YES	NOT YET	IDEAS
Norms have been developed.			
The platform has been identified.			
A technology and logistics person has been identified.			
An emotional check-in or other kickoff has been identified.			
The purpose for the session is clear.			
There are frequent low-stakes interactions planned.			
Breakout room discussion questions have been developed.			
Questions and feedback from the group are posed.			
Breaks are scheduled.			
Reflections are interspersed.			
There is a plan to solicit feedback about the content of the session.			

LEARNING

SAFE PRACTICE

It is amazing how hard teachers can be on themselves when it comes to their own learning. Nearly every teacher will readily tell you about the importance of creating opportunities for their students to try new skills in a low-stakes environment. Educators understand that there is value in giving students time to struggle a bit, and that this struggle is productive because it results in new conceptual understandings. After all, they will explain, if opportunities for practice and refinement weren't important, we could just lecture and call it a day. Yet when it comes to their own learning, they can be quite unforgiving. If they aren't perfect from the start, they beat themselves up about it.

We get that. None of us relishes trying out something new and having it go in an unexpected direction. Distance learning in general has certainly been an example of the steep learning curve we have all had to scale. But there can be added and unnecessary pressure when the pace of professional learning fails to allow time for safe practice. By that, we mean a window of time for teachers to try out something new and experiment with it. With safe practice, there isn't a fear of judgment in front of others. Instead, it's a chance to rehearse and reflect before engaging with other colleagues and administrators. Think of it as a trial period. It is an important yet often overlooked step in professional learning.

Safe practice is the linchpin that occurs between the initial knowledge acquisition presented in one or more formal professional development sessions and the follow-up microevents at the grade, department, or classroom levels. These follow-ups are crucial, of course, and often consist of coaching and engaging with peers. However, this quiet period provides teachers with the psychological space to experiment as they take on a new approach.

MAKE IT ACTIONABLE

Develop your professional learning cycle such that it includes a period of safe practice. As a school leader, you want to be able to amplify emerging practices. But these are unlikely to take hold if there isn't an opportunity to try out new ideas in a psychologically safe way. It's a "culture of error" that acknowledges the essential nature of learning through failed and partially successful attempts (Mourão, 2018, p. 132). By building an environment that is conducive to adult learning, you strengthen the commitment of teachers to the school and to one another.

NOTE TO SELF

What dimensions of safe practice do you currently have in place? Assess current professional learning at your site and identify areas to strengthen adult learning.

	CURRENTLY DOING	PLANNING TO DO	TO CONSIDER
Protected time is built into the professional development calendar.			
Teachers have opportunities to try new practices in a low-stakes environment.			
Teachers are not observed by an administrator during the time when they are trying a new practice.			

VIRTUAL LEARNING WALKS

The third-grade team at Arroyo Vista elementary school visited the classrooms of their fourth-grade colleagues. This school has had learning walks in place for many years. As they transitioned to distance learning, the teams requested that the learning walks continue. As a fifth-grade teacher noted, "We learn so much from seeing others impact students' learning. And there is so much to learn in distance learning. I want to see everything that I can." The five third-grade teachers joined the synchronous session of one of the fourth-grade teachers' classroom. They were added to breakout rooms to observe students. The students had just read an article about the Gold Rush and were sharing their key ideas. After about eight minutes, the third-grade teachers left this room and visited another classroom. In this classroom, the students had finished their collaborative conversations and were sharing their summary statements. The visitors observed for about seven minutes before moving to the next classroom. In that classroom, they observed students writing and sharing their writing with one another and the teacher. The students in this class submitted their work in the chat and the teacher invited students to read their writing aloud, seeking feedback from peers.

ESSENTIAL QUESTION: How can colleagues learn from one another's practice at a distance?

YOUR GOAL: Implement virtual learning walks to facilitate collaborative learning.

As one of the third-grade teachers noted, "I had not thought about using the chat to have students transfer pictures of their work to me. It's so easy. I'm so glad we were able to see that. I am going to use that tomorrow."

Another member of the third-grade team added, "I really liked seeing the students collaborate. The language they were using was great. I think that the process was really good to see. I think we need to talk about some common routines that we can use with our students when they are in breakout rooms. I think that we could build more language with them if they had clearer expectations."

The conversation continued with ideas gleaned from their virtual walk through. At this school, teams visit other teachers biweekly as part of their collaboration time. They visit different grade levels with different purposes. But the idea is that they look for ideas that impact students' learning.

Watching each other in action is one of the best ways for teachers to benefit from each other's practices. Yet for all our good intentions, it is quite difficult to find time to spend in each other's physical classrooms. Teaching at a distance can breed a sense of isolation and disconnection from colleagues. Teachers in distance learning or otherwise need tools that allow them to maximize the supportive structures created to foster collective teacher efficacy (Hord, 1997).

Virtual learning walks are planned and coordinated classroom visits that focus on the common challenge agreed upon by the group. That's a really important point. There is a narrow focus on one agreed purpose, not on looking at everything that is happening. They have much in common with instructional rounds (City, Elmore, Fiarman, & Tietel, 2009), although they are less formal and more varied. Teaching teams complete a series of short joint observations of synchronous or asynchronous lessons (typically five to ten minutes in length) to gain a sense of the patterns noticed. These are not classroom observations in the conventional sense of the term. First, they are not evaluative. This can be a difficult habit to break, as stating that something is "good" or "effective" is evaluative. Rather, the purpose is to gather objective data focused on a specific common challenge ("I noticed that the students I observed in the breakout room referred to their weekly goals sheets.") and then to organize those observations into patterns. See Figure 2.3 for a chart of the types of learning walks and their purposes.

Virtual ghost walks are done in the absence of students, and focus on the physical environment, in this case the learning management system (LMS). For example, a fourth-grade team who has identified academic language use as a common challenge might conduct a virtual ghost walk of each other's LMS to look for patterns of environmental support for language use, such as the presence of language frames and target vocabulary on asynchronous tasks. Teachers simply share their screen and give a guided tour of where these items are posted in the LMS.

Capacity-building virtual learning walks are conducted within and across teams. The classroom visits are scheduled in advance with volunteer teachers and focus on a specific common challenge. The middle school math team profiled in this section used capacity-building learning walks to learn from one another about new ways to foster algebraic thinking. An elementary school with the common

Figure 2.3   Virtual Learning Walks and Their Purposes

Type of Walk	Purpose	Time	Participants	Follow-Up After the Walk
Virtual Ghost Walk	To examine learning management systems (LMS) for elements of asynchronous learning. Teachers volunteer to make their LMS available and in turn are participants in the virtual ghost walk as they view others.	1 hour	Members of the professional learning community	*Summary of data collected:* Evidence and wonderings processed within the PLC+ team, or across other professional learning communities
Virtual Capacity-Building Learning Walks	This walk focuses solely on collecting data to inform decisions in synchronous or asynchronous environments. Collection of data and evidence help identify the implementation of effective practices and gain insights into next steps.	2 hours	Members of the building leadership team, in partnership with members of the professional learning communities	*Summary of data collected:* Evidence and wonderings processed within the PLC+ team, or with entire faculty
Virtual Faculty Learning Walks	The goal of this type of learning walk is to focus on the learning of the entire teaching staff. It involves all teachers in visiting other teachers' classroom outside of the PLC+ to which members belong. This can spark new ideas and strategies for teachers to incorporate into their own practice.	A series of scheduled sessions over the course of a week	Principal, assistant principal, members of the building leadership team, and whoever is available each period and/or time segment, ultimately involving entire faculty throughout the year	*Summary of data collected:* Evidence and wonderings processed with entire faculty

Source: Adapted from Fisher, D., Frey, N., Almarode, J., Flories, K., & Nagel, D. (2020b). *The PLC+ playbook: A hands-on guide to collectively improving student learning* (p. 89). Thousand Oaks, CA: Corwin. Used with permission.

challenge of increasing the emotional regulation skills of their students used a series of cross-grade-level capacity-building learning walks to learn about the work of colleagues in this effort with students of different ages. In both cases, they briefly joined a series of synchronous sessions to gain a sense of how their colleagues are implementing an instructional approach.

Instructional leadership teams measure, monitor, and modify professional learning efforts using *virtual faculty learning walks*. Their task is to look for patterns and trends regarding the current focus of the professional learning cycle. These teams comprise school leaders and teacher leaders, who work together to make decisions about the direction of the professional learning. Each professional learning cycle is ten weeks in length but is subject to the findings of these faculty learning walks. It is not uncommon for an ILT to determine that additional learning is warranted, and that the next round of professional learning should be a continuation of the work, not an entirely new focus. This decision-making method empowers teachers and school leaders to make evidence-based informed choices about professional learning.

Planning for learning walks is crucial. Given that the observations are short, it is important to arrive at an agreed common challenge in advance. Lacking a focus, groups have a tendency to look at everything (and therefore nothing) in an attempt to take in the whole. But a short virtual classroom visit is a snapshot, and nothing more. No one would indiscriminately take photos using their smartphone camera that were devoid of any purpose or composition. Wandering in and out of virtual sessions or looking randomly at a bunch of LMS examples without a focus is equally unproductive. The planned nature of virtual learning walks means that teachers are able to plan aligned experiences timed to the schedule, thus allowing teams to witness what they came to see.

MAKE IT ACTIONABLE

Whether brick-and-mortar or virtual, schools as organizations need ways to learn. Virtual learning walks provide schools with tools to amplify emerging practices and gauge growth in a focus area. The use of virtual learning walks continues to reinforce an important message to teachers about the collective wisdom of the group and continuing efforts to build opportunities for meaningful collaboration.

NOTE TO SELF

In what ways do teaching teams contribute to the collaborative learning of the school? Assess current professional learning at your site and identify areas of collaboration beyond planning times.

	CURRENTLY DOING	PLANNING TO DO	TO CONSIDER
Teams schedule time to share asynchronous methods that are aligned to the professional learning focus.			
Teams schedule time to observe each other's synchronous methods that are aligned to the professional learning focus.			
The instructional leadership team joins with other teachers to conduct virtual learning walks to monitor progress on the professional learning focus.			

Microteaching is the practice of capturing a portion of a lesson or student interaction on video for the purpose of analyzing it. These are teacher-directed coaching events from inception to discussion with the professional learning community. The content usually focuses on the common challenge identified by the team. This is particularly easy to accomplish in distance learning. A volunteer teacher records a synchronous session of themself then views it individually to identify a segment to share with their team. The volunteer teacher sets the context of the segment for their colleagues and poses their questions. After viewing, the team asks questions meant to mediate the thinking of the volunteer teacher. The questions should not be thinly veiled evaluations or suggestions but rather are designed to spark the thinking of the volunteer teacher. Suggested open-ended questions for the team include (Fisher et al., 2020a, p. 98):

- What did you want your students to know and be able to do?
- What connections have you made?
- What did you see or hear that confirms your previous thinking?
- What did you see or hear that conflicts with your previous thinking?
- Which moments did you find to be particularly effective?
- Which moments did you think did not go as well as you had hoped?
- What was different in comparing those moments?
- What would you change in order to accomplish your stated goal?
- What do you want to be sure to do again?

Microteaching, properly implemented, is a significant influencer on student achievement, with an effect size of 0.88 (Hattie, 2020). In addition, microteaching fosters collective teacher efficacy through relational trust, observational learning, and social cohesion. See Figure 2.4 for a comparison of what microteaching is and is not.

ESSENTIAL QUESTION: How can teachers provide collegial coaching to one another when they are at a distance?

YOUR GOAL: Foster collaborative professional learning through microteaching.

Deanna Trejo, a high school history teacher, volunteered to share a video clip from her class at their team meeting. She selected a clip that focused on her demonstrating her thinking during asynchronous learning. Her team had been focused on teacher modeling and creating interactive videos, which has an effect size of 0.54. The video clip focused on Ms. Trejo reading from a primary source document and sharing her thinking with students. At one point in the lesson, Ms. Trejo asks herself a question and then the video pauses and students are required to type in a question that is in their minds about the text. Later in the clip,

LEARNING

Figure 2.4 A Comparison of Microteaching Practices

What Microteaching *Is*		What Microteaching *Is Not*
To co-construct content pedagogical knowledge with the team	**Purpose**	To evaluate someone else's teaching
Identified by the teacher	**Determination of Focus**	Identified by others
Directs the discussion	**Role of the Teacher**	Listens passively
To ask mediating questions to prompt the thinking of the teacher	**Role of Other PLC+ Members**	To provide feedback about the quality of the lesson; to offer judgments and personal opinions

Source: Fisher et al. (2020b). *The PLC+ playbook: A hands-on guide to collectively improving student learning* (p. 89). Thousand Oaks, CA: Corwin. Used with permission.

Ms. Trejo makes a connection between the text she is reading and another text that the class had read during a synchronous lesson.

As a team, the history teachers discussed the video clip. At one point, they asked about what did not go as well as planned. Ms. Trejo said, "I think that sometimes I make it seem like there is only one way to think about the text. I think that's the same as when we were in physical school, but seeing it in video makes me think about it more. I want students to work through their understanding of the text. I want them to think about bias and perspective. I think that I need to focus on that during my modeling."

The conversation continued about how teachers could integrate various perspectives and the idea that often there were many right answers and some wrong answers when it came to analyzing primary source documents. At the end of the session, one of the teachers said, "I'm so glad we take time to do this. It's really helping me think about how I can create lessons that push the thinking of our students."

MAKE IT ACTIONABLE

Although microteaching as a practice has been used for decades, it may not be known to the teachers at your school. Introduce them to the process of microteaching as another tool to support their professional learning. Figure 2.5 is a protocol we developed for the process. Introduce this protocol at your school and follow up with teachers about their impressions and its usefulness.

Figure 2.5 Microteaching Protocol

Before Filming	
What are my goals for this process? (e.g., to improve a teaching technique, to refine my ability to engage in expert noticing, to identify the thinking of a student)	
When will I record the lesson? Who will I need for assistance before, during, or after the recording?	
What do I hope to capture in the video?	
After Filming	
Schedule time to review the footage. In what ways was the lesson you delivered different from the lesson you planned?	
What questions does the recording raise for you?	
What questions do you want your team to help you answer?	
In Your Team Meeting	
Introduce the video to your team, set the context, and pose your major questions.	

(Continued)

(Continued)

In Your Team Meeting
Suggested team member questions

- What did you want your students to know and be able to do?
- What connections have you made?
- What did you see or hear that confirms your previous thinking?
- What did you see or hear that conflicts with your previous thinking?
- Which moments did you find to be particularly effective?
- Which moments did you think did not go as well as you had hoped?
- What was different in comparing those moments?
- What would you change in order to accomplish your stated goal?
- What do you want to be sure to do again?

Debrief the Microteaching Experience as a Whole	
What did we learn today as a team?	
How might we move student learning forward?	
How might we move our own learning forward?	
What goals do we have for ourselves for the next two weeks?	

Source: Adapted from Fisher et al. (2020b). *The PLC+ playbook: A hands-on guide to collectively improving student learning* (p. 96). Thousand Oaks, CA: Corwin. Used with permission.

 Available for download at **resources.corwin.com/DLPlaybook-leaders**

PERSONALIZED PROFESSIONAL LEARNING

The demands of distance learning have attenuated the real-time needs of educators to learn new tools and approaches quickly. But it can be challenging to a school leader to try to provide a course for professional learning that will meet the needs of all teachers. Round out schoolwide cycles of inquiry and grade- or department-level microevents with personalized learning that is directed by the individual.

The job-embedded nature of personalized learning allows teachers to direct their own course for learning in ways that afford an immediate benefit to their classroom practice. A teacher might join a personal learning network (PLN) of like-minded educators from across the globe who meet virtually to discuss ideas and trade resources. There are any number of Twitter chats, virtual book clubs, and even formal courses that focus on a unique subject. Early evidence on personalized approaches to professional learning is that it increases job satisfaction (Morrison, 2019). This approach has been especially appealing to educators who do not have other job-alike partners in the school, such as the media specialist, art, music, and physical education teachers, and the school counselor. Their use of a PLN that extends outside of the school gives them the opportunity to expand their subject and pedagogical knowledge.

At the school where three of us work, we have encouraged teachers in past years to form their own PLNs to explore a topic in more depth. The networks meet twice a year to share their practices with others and then reconfigure each time. Many stay with the same PLN, while others move to a new network because they are interested in what they heard. Teachers reported that they valued what they were learning because of the self-initiated nature and the opportunity to exercise choice, another key principle of adult learning (Knowles, 1970).

ESSENTIAL QUESTION: How can our organization meet the distance learning needs of every teacher?

YOUR GOAL: Foster a culture of personalized learning for every teacher and administrator.

MAKE IT ACTIONABLE

Learn about the interests of teachers at your school by hosting individual meetings with each to discuss their personalized learning for the year. Effective teachers are continuously building their own capacities but are less commonly recognized for the learning they conduct on their own. By knowing what it is that each teacher is interested in pursuing, you obtain a more nuanced understanding of the people you work with. In addition, you can assist in building informal networks among the staff, especially in pairing those with similar learning goals. Figure 2.6 is a suggested discussion frame for teachers to complete in advance of meeting with you.

Figure 2.6 Personalized Learning Plan

Proposal for Personalized Professional Learning	
What is your personal learning goal for this school year?	I want to learn about _____. I want to strengthen my practice _____. I want to teach others about _____.
How will you know you have been successful in achieving your goal?	
How will you demonstrate evidence of your learning?	

What specific professional learning experiences will you utilize?	
Online course	Date range
Webinars	Date(s)
Content repository	Name(s)
E-learning platforms (e.g., Twitter Education Chats, Facebook Live broadcasts, district social media interest groups)	Name(s)
Coaching-intensive platform	Date range
Who is your accountability partner?	
Is there a financial cost?	

 Available for download at **resources.corwin.com/DLPlaybook-leaders**

SOCIAL PRESENCE

It can be a challenge to provide feedback to staff members in a virtual environment. The human-to-human interactions we normally use rely on establishing closeness between participants. We accomplish these through many nonverbal behaviors, including eye contact and facial expressions. These are further enacted by mirroring the actions of the other person, such as adopting similar gestures, body positions, and language. We do this subconsciously, through complex neurological processes that help us understand the emotions of the other person. It can be a bit more difficult to do so when you are meeting with a teacher in a virtual setting. Both of you are reduced to a thumbnail box image, typically from the shoulders up. The lighting and the audio quality can further interfere with the communication channel.

Social presence in an online environment is the degree to which one person perceives that they are interacting with a "real" person (Garrison et al., 2000). We don't mean to suggest that either of you are delusional. On an intellectual level, we know the other person in a virtual meeting isn't a robot. But much of what we process through communication is not conscious. As humans we are continuously monitoring the emotional, affective, and sensory information we detect, not only the content of the message. A person's ability to understand and apply information is enhanced when they have a higher degree of social presence. The good news is that our behavior can positively contribute to a person's feeling of being socially present with you, even at a distance. These behaviors are expressed across five dimensions (Sung & Mayer, 2012). Think of these as ways in which you transmit a sense of caring and warmth that bridges the physical distance of your interactions.

When paired with the behaviors that increase your social presence, you increase the ability of the teacher to receive your coaching and feedback and act upon it.

> **ESSENTIAL QUESTION:** How can I overcome the communication barriers that make coaching and feedback more challenging?
>
> **YOUR GOAL:** Enhance your social presence to build professional relationships.

MAKE IT ACTIONABLE

People who feel a lack of social connection in an online environment are less likely to feel motivated to interact or to accept feedback. This is true of students and it is true of the adults you work with. Your improved social presence in virtual environments, coupled with microfeedback that is timely, growth oriented, and sought out, serve your coaching and supervision responsibilities well.

LEARNING

Figure 2.7 Improving Your Social Presence

Indicators	Examples That Contribute to Increased Social Presence
Social Respect	• Expressions of appreciation • Acknowledgment of ideas, opinions, or points of view • Timely response
Social Sharing	• Sharing information • Relational trust • A close relationship
Social Identity	• Greeting the person • Using the person's name
Open Mind	• Expressing agreement or disagreement about ideas productively • Offering positive feedback • Disclosures about self
Intimacy	• Expressing personal experiences • Expressing emotions and feelings

NOTE TO SELF

Plan your next micro-feedback meeting with a teacher. How will you enhance your social presence? After the meeting, self-assess whether you were successful.

INDICATOR	HOW WILL YOU DO THIS?	DID YOU ACCOMPLISH THIS?
Social Respect		
Social Sharing		
Social Identity		
Open mind		
Intimacy		

PARENT EDUCATION AND SUPPORT

We are not asking parents to be their child's history teacher (or any other teacher for that matter). Instead, we are hoping that they can support the learning that is occurring from a distance, recognizing that there are differences in the realities that families face. Some people are working multiple jobs, others are essential workers, and still others are looking for work. As a school leader, your communication with family members is critical and establishes the baseline expectations. And, your understanding of the various situations for families in the community needs to come through in the communication you send home.

But to say that families are too busy, or too poor, or simply unable to help negates the fact that parents and other relatives really do want the children in their lives to learn. The messages you send should reinforce the belief you have that parents want the best for their children. You should also be careful about sending messages that imply that they are not "good" parents if they don't have hours on end to reteach the content.

In *The Distance Learning Playbook for Parents* (Wiseman, Fisher, Frey, & Hattie, 2020), we noted that there are some basic routines that can be implemented to improve the likelihood that learning will occur. We have noted the importance of regular and sufficient sleep, a dedicated place to learn, morning routines to be ready for school, the integration of movement and exercise into the day, and communicating with teachers. Regular messages to family members about these basics are important.

In addition, there are ways that parents can help the teacher create a productive learning environment. Here are some of the messages that leaders have found useful:

> **ESSENTIAL QUESTION:** How have you supported parents to partner with teachers in their children's education?
>
> **YOUR GOAL:** Ensure that parents understand how to help.

- **Struggle**. It's okay to allow your child to struggle. In fact, productive struggle is good for their brains and their learning. Please do not do the work for your child or tell them the answers. You can provide hints as your child practices, but please understand that struggle is part of the learning experience. If your child struggles too much, let the teacher know and we'll schedule some additional small-group time. We know that you want to help but telling them the answers actually robs them of the learning experience.

- **Privacy to take risks**. Step away from your child's learning environment on a regular basis and allow your child to be wrong, to make mistakes, to take risks. Errors are opportunities to learn and the teacher needs to know which errors your child makes so that they can design appropriate lessons.

- **Read a lot**. Reading volume is highly related to overall achievement. Reading a lot builds background knowledge and vocabulary. Effective schools have students read about ninety minutes per day. Make sure that your child is reading a lot to allow the instruction to stick.

- **Practice.** Practice does not make perfect, but it does make permanent. If you have time to help your child, allocate time to support their practice. The teacher will assign practice. The goal is not to just "get it done" but rather to apply what you have learned to these tasks. In fact, children need to overlearn at the beginning so that they can do things automatically.

- **Talk about learning.** Try not to ask your child what they did today during school and instead focus on what they learned. Ask your child, "Did you ask an interesting question today?" Talk about the learning and encourage your child to teach what they learned to members of the family. You might even record these teach-back sessions for the teacher to see what your child remembered.

- **Know what they are learning.** When the teacher talks about what the class is learning, try to take note and bring it up later. For example, if the class is focused on ending punctuation, ask your child to notice the punctuation on common items such as the cereal box. If the class is learning about fractions, have the child help measure using cups that have to be combined to get the right amount. It will help us if you have any time to have your child practice what they are learning.

- **Know the learning management system.** There are a number of tools that teachers use in distance learning. These tools allow children to find things such as assignments and they allow children to submit their work. Learn a little about the system used so that you can assist your child when the teacher is not available.

MAKE IT ACTIONABLE

Develop a plan to regularly communicate with family members about the ways that they can support their children. Be clear that you are not asking them to be the teacher, but rather to support the learning that their children are doing. Family members access information in a variety of ways. How can you use the following tools to communicate with family members? Perhaps there are some tools that you choose to use and others that you don't. We're not suggesting that you need to use them all. But you probably want to focus on several ways of sharing information.

NOTE TO SELF

Which tools do you have that you can use to communicate with families?

TOOL	COMMON FUNCTION	MY PLAN FOR USE
School website	Organize resources and information	
Remind (or other messaging app)	Send short messages that convey "just-in-time" information	
Webinars	Provide topical information such as college applications or family math	
Twitter	Broadcast messages to the community of followers	
Facebook or Instagram	Capture the spirit of the organization	
Virtual office hours	Provide interaction opportunities	

LEARNING

3 INSTRUCTIONAL LEADERSHIP AT A DISTANCE

The experiences that teachers plan for students should ensure that learning occurs. There are any number of "right" ways to teach. We do not believe in prescribing teaching methods. As we will explore further in the mindframes section of this book, we focus on learning. Having said that, there are ineffective ways to engage students that do not result in deep learning. As a leader, you have the potential to support teachers in the selection and implementation of effective approaches to ensure that learning occurs.

In this section:

☐ REVISIT SCHOOL GOALS IN LIGHT OF DISTANCE LEARNING

☐ ALIGN GOALS TO EXPECTATIONS

☐ CLARIFY TEACHER EXPECTATIONS

☐ ENSURE CULTURALLY SUSTAINING PEDAGOGIES

☐ USE A DISTANCE LEARNING INSTRUCTIONAL FRAMEWORK

☐ DEMONSTRATING IN DISTANCE LEARNING

☐ COLLABORATING IN DISTANCE LEARNING

☐ COACHING AND FACILITATING IN DISTANCE LEARNING

☐ PRACTICING IN DISTANCE LEARNING

SCHOOL
LEADERS
CAN HAVE A
TREMENDOUS
POSITIVE
IMPACT ON
THE LEARNING
LIVES OF
STUDENTS.

School leaders can have a tremendous positive impact on the learning lives of students. Notice that we said *can*. Student learning is impacted both directly and indirectly by the efforts of school leaders as they coordinate the instructional efforts of the teaching staff, build a positive school climate, work with families, and enact the school's vision and mission.

The type of leadership employed matters. Robinson, Lloyd, and Rowe (2008) examined the impact of two leadership styles—transformational and instructional—on student learning. Their reported results are interesting and nuanced. Their headline-grabbing finding is that instructional leadership has an effect size of 0.42, while transformational leadership has a much smaller impact on student learning, at 0.11. But their quantitative results should be interpreted with some thoughtful caveats. The constant is student learning, so it makes sense that instructional leadership would have a stronger impact. Therefore, transformational leadership, which has more of a focus on staff relations, would of course be less. Overall, they reported five dimensions of instructional leadership that had the highest degree of impact:

- *Establishing goals and expectations* to focus the efforts of teachers and students.

- *Resourcing strategically* to secure resources aligned to instructional efforts.

- *Planning, coordinating, and evaluating teaching across the curriculum* that includes collegial conversations, observations, and formative feedback.

- *Promoting and participating in teacher learning and professional development,* rather than simply sponsoring it.

- *Ensuring an orderly and supportive environment* so that academic goals can be achieved.

The authors note that "the closer educational leaders get to the core business of teaching and learning, the more likely they are to have a positive impact on students' outcomes" (p. 664). They go on to point out that the context of the school matters in making decisions about where one's efforts should be placed. If the needs of the school are first and foremost about orderliness and civility, then one's efforts should be oriented there. Nor should there be a misinterpretation that an effective school leader must perform at high levels at all times in all five dimensions, which reinforces the "highly problematic heroic approach to school leadership" (p. 668).

Middle school principal Sandra Richardson is figuring out how to convert her instructional leadership practices in a distance learning environment. "When we have been in physical school, I block off two hours a day on my calendar to walk classrooms. Sometimes it's with another administrator, or with some of the teacher–leaders." However, she has struggled to find ways to do that virtually. "I've finally gotten a schedule together for myself to visit classrooms during live sessions. I use Symbaloo but others in our district use other options," she said. "I'm only there for a few minutes, but it is proving to be a good payoff in terms of knowing what's going on in the school. I can't just walk down the hall and get a sense. So I'm figuring out how to normalize my presence in virtual classrooms for the students and the staff." In doing so, Ms. Richardson is prioritizing her instructional leadership efforts.

DRAWING ON MY EXPERTISE

Think about the current context of your school during distance learning. Use the traffic light scale to reflect on your practices as a school leader. To what extent is each of these statements true?

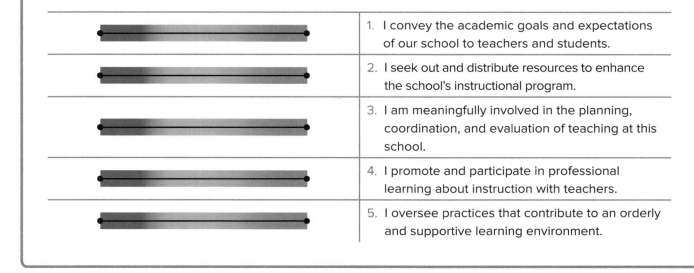

Scale	Statement
	1. I convey the academic goals and expectations of our school to teachers and students.
	2. I seek out and distribute resources to enhance the school's instructional program.
	3. I am meaningfully involved in the planning, coordination, and evaluation of teaching at this school.
	4. I promote and participate in professional learning about instruction with teachers.
	5. I oversee practices that contribute to an orderly and supportive learning environment.

REVISIT SCHOOL GOALS IN LIGHT OF DISTANCE LEARNING

The academic goals of the school are at the heart of any school improvement plan. Much research has been conducted over the last few decades on the development of school goals. Because schools are relatively stable environments, goal planning, implementation, and monitoring tend to be articulated over multiple years. It's not uncommon to see school goals that include a three-year plan. But who talks about what you're supposed to do when everything changes?

It turns out that high-risk industries such as aviation and energy do. Accidents in these industries can be catastrophic, so most firms have Health, Safety, Security, and Environment (HSSE) plans. The purpose is to lead through the crisis and not just manage the response. McNulty and Marcus (2020), founders of the National Preparedness Leadership Initiative

> **ESSENTIAL QUESTION:** To what extent do the school goals we currently have reflect our needs in distance learning?
>
> **YOUR GOAL:** Use a process to identify a starting point to jumpstart your collaboration with your instructional leadership team.

at Harvard, caution that a mistake is to overcentralize the response and try to control everything yourself. "The solution is to seek order rather than control," they advise.

The school's goals can be the rocket fuel that propels learning, or they can be the sand in the gears that brings everything to a halt. When instructional goals are viewed by the staff as being punitive, or when they have not had a role in developing them, their value is about as much as the paper they're printed on. In moving forward from pandemic teaching to a more coherent distance learning environment, you will probably need to revisit instructional goals.

But resist the temptation to rewrite goals without collaboration or to just ignore the existing ones altogether. Your instructional leadership team is even more valuable to you now than ever before. But they also need direction from you on how to get started. Your willingness to reexamine instructional goals in light of changing circumstances sends an important message of stability. In addition, it signals a return to the core mission of schooling: the education of young people.

MAKE IT ACTIONABLE

"I used the AC/DC plan to begin the conversation about refining our school's goals," said high school principal Mykal Chambers. "Add, Change, Delete, or Continue." Dr. Chambers and the administrative and teaching staff had developed instructional goals in 2019. "Then everything changed, and we had to look again at our plans." The principal said that the process gave them an opportunity to determine what they needed to prioritize. "We were actually pleasantly surprised that the majority of our goals still worked in distance learning." Use the Note to Self to take a preliminary inventory of your school's instructional goals. Extend this by using this as a tool to survey members of your instructional leadership team to gain their insights to identify where any revisions need to occur.

List up to five major instructional goals your school has. Consider those in the context of distance learning. Are there any that need to be changed, deleted, or continued as is?

	CHANGE?	DELETE?	CONTINUE?
1.			
2.			
3.			
4.			
5.			

POSSIBLE GOALS TO ADD

LEADERSHIP

ALIGN GOALS TO EXPECTATIONS

ESSENTIAL QUESTION: Are the instructional goals of the school aligned to expectations for distance learning?

YOUR GOAL: Communicate expectations to staff with distance learning in mind.

Organizations use expectations to foster consistency and instill confidence in their staff. Expectations begin with job descriptions, but don't end there. After all, when was the last time you looked at your official job description? The move to distance learning has probably created some disequilibrium for certificated and classified staff. In some cases, their job expectations may have shifted due to distance learning. Unifying the staff in order to perpetuate the core mission of the school—student learning—can be a challenge when adults are not interacting in the ways they have been accustomed. The Institute for Organization Management, the professional development initiative of the U.S. Chamber of Commerce, says that setting expectations can be beneficial across six dimensions:

- *Clarity.* When expectations are discussed and unpacked, you and the staff can get on the same page. Every rower knows that all the oars in the water need to be pulling in the same direction.

- *Baseline for measurement.* Instructional leadership requires communication, feedback, and goal setting. But when staff aren't clear on how their efforts contribute to the mission of the school, performance can suffer. Clear expectations equip staff with the calibration tools they need to guide their own performance.

- *Communication.* Stated expectations provide staff members with a common vocabulary of excellence.

- *Empowerment.* Expectations are not intended to be onerous, or to ensnare people in a game of "gotcha." Empowered staff are better able to make decisions that are consistent with guidelines. After all, you don't want everyone coming to you about every decision.

- *A reference point when expectations aren't met.* A staff member who struggles is a staff member in need of feedback. But feedback is much more difficult when the expectations haven't been clearly stated and enacted.

- *Supports accountability to self and the school.* Formal performance reviews are conducted as articulated by contracts and bargaining agreements. But all of us operate on another level of informal accountability to ourselves and to the school.

Above all, clear expectations convey assurance for all the members of the staff and demonstrate your confidence in them. During a time of disruption, expectations can be a steadying factor for all involved.

MAKE IT ACTIONABLE

At the school where three of us work, we pride ourselves on being a school that learns by using experiences as a fulcrum to always improve from within (Senge, Cambron-McCabe, Lucas, Smith, & Dutton, 2012). Each year, we revisit and update our school expectations with the staff in order to reflect the collective wisdom of the school community. Their voices are an essential component of the expectations we hold for ourselves and as a school community. While the categories remain the same, the details of each of them get refined as a product of growth. In a time of distance learning, the staff has revised them to mirror the next normal in our practices. The true value is on the conversations we have as an organization, as it becomes a way to clarify, seek understanding, and continue to improve. Use the categories as a starting point for detailing the distance learning expectations at your school. You can draft expectations and then host staff discussion to finalize yours.

Distance Learning Expectations	
Records	**Supervision**
• Learning logs reflect 4 hours of student work each day (90 minutes in live instruction) and are accurate, complete, and timely. • Attendance each period is accurate and timely. • Grade books are updated at least twice weekly. • Student work is returned within one week. • Routine paperwork and substitute plans are completed on time.	• The well-being of each student is a collective responsibility. We advocate on behalf of any student who faces challenges related to access, mental wellness, or other circumstances, regardless of professional position. • We collaborate with the Attendance, Re-engagement, and Career Development Teams to mobilize supports. • Attendance at virtual extracurricular activities occurs regularly. • Student behavior is monitored and feedback about their citizenship is provided.
Instruction	**Curriculum**
• Daily content, language, and social purposes are posted on the LMS. Students know the criteria for success. • Teacher modeling occurs in each lesson, synchronously or asynchronously. • Student collaboration is extensive and occurs in each daily live session. • Formal and informal assessments are used formatively to guide instruction.	• Lessons, both live and asynchronous, are rigorous, systematic and planned, and based on state content and language development standards. • Units are appropriately interdisciplinary and linked to relevant topics and/or health content. • Weekly deliberate practice is consistent and rigorous.

(Continued)

LEADERSHIP

(Continued)

Instruction (continued)	Curriculum (continued)
• Small group instruction and intervention occurs regularly. • Students read, write, and speak daily across every live and asynchronous lesson. • Targeted instruction and language supports are provided to English learners. • Homework is used formatively (review, fluency, application, extension).	• Assessments and grading are competency based. • Honors contracts are offered and executed. • Feature-length films are used minimally, judiciously, and are preapproved. Short films include vocabulary and/or writing activities.
Communication	**Professional Learning**
• Choice words and nonverbal cues are used to build each student's agency and identity. • Parents, students, and colleagues receive responses within one workday. • Departments, grade-levels, and student support staff members interact regularly in virtual environments using affective statements and growth-producing approaches. • Restorative practices are used to resolve conflict and repair harm. Follow-up is used to build students' agency.	• Every adult is a learner and a teacher. • Coaching is essential to learning, and everyone is coached. • Professional development is essential to continuous improvement and takes priority over other professional obligations. • We keep our cameras on whenever possible in order to promote our collective communication and learning. • Virtual classrooms are welcoming of visitors who also help us to learn more about ourselves.
Student Support	**Peer Support**
• Teachers host virtual office hours weekly. • Proactive engagement with students about their attendance, performance, language development, and recovery needs is ongoing. • Social and emotional learning is infused in lessons. • Attendance at, and participation in, virtual IEP meetings occurs regularly. • Students are spotlighted for positive accomplishments and areas of concern. • Appropriate interventions are implemented.	• Honest, humane, and growth-producing conversations occur regularly. • Choice words are used to build agency and identity between and among staff. • Mentoring and coaching relationships are supportive and ongoing. • Each adult does whatever it takes to ensure the success of others. • Successes and achievements are celebrated. • Asking for help is a sign of strength, not weakness.

NOTE TO SELF

What distance learning expectations might you consider in each of these categories? Partner with your instructional leadership team to draft expectations. Share these draft ideas with your staff to co-construct expectations together.

Records	
Supervision	
Instruction	
Curriculum	
Communication	
Professional Learning	
Student Support	
Peer Support	

LEADERSHIP

CLARIFY TEACHER EXPECTATIONS

ESSENTIAL QUESTION: How do teacher expectations impact student learning?

YOUR GOAL: Ensure that teachers hold high expectations for all students.

Teachers hold expectations for their students. By right, teachers should have high expectations for all of their students. Interestingly, the effect size of teacher expectations is not that strong, with an effect size of 0.43. Clearly there are many other things that influence a student's learning beyond the expectations the teacher holds for the learner. In fact, students' expectations of themselves, as expressed in their ability to predict their performance or grade, is much higher with an effect size of 1.33.

The question is, do you know if teachers have high expectations for their students? All of them? And what will you do if you notice that a teacher has low expectations? The expectations that teachers have for students develops, in part, based on the relationships that teachers and students form. People learn better when they have a positive relationship with the person providing instruction. Elements of teacher–student relationships include (Cornelius-White, 2007, p. 113)

- *Teacher empathy*—understanding
- *Unconditional positive regard*—warmth
- *Genuineness*—the teacher's self-awareness
- *Nondirectivity*—student-initiated and student-regulated activities
- *Encouragement of critical thinking* as opposed to traditional memory emphasis

NOTE TO SELF

How do teachers in your school establish (or reestablish) relationships with students in a distance learning environment? We've started a list for you. How will you personalize it to your context?

Teacher Empathy *How do students seek connections with teachers?*	• Begin synchronous and asynchronous lessons with a positive affirmation (e.g., favorite quotes, a silly joke, short video messages). • Establish virtual office hours for students to drop in for academic support. • Host short check-in conferences with families and the student to see how they are doing and what they need. • •
Unconditional Positive Regard *How do students know teachers care about them as people?*	• Weave into lessons what you have learned about students' pursuits through interest surveys. • Provide polls for students to respond to at the end of class meetings. • Use voice feedback tools on student work so they can hear the sparkle in your voice, rather than read your words without context. • •
Genuineness *How will students know teachers care about themselves as a professional?*	• Dress and groom professionally. • Project a demeanor that is optimistic about them and you. • Make it clear in words and actions that this is a place for learning about themselves, the world, and each other. • •
Nondirectivity *How will students know teachers hold their abilities in high regard?*	• Hold individual conversations with students to help them identify their strengths, goals, and growth areas. • Ask questions that mediate the student's thinking, rather than ask leading questions. • Use shared decision making about curriculum with students. • •
Encouragement of Critical Thinking *Are students asked critical thinking questions?*	• Foster discussion among peers using questions that open up their thinking. • Every distance learning session includes opportunities for students to write about, illustrate, or discuss their thinking with peers. • Build choice and relevance into assignments and projects. • •

LEADERSHIP

These student-centered practices are essential in any classroom, perhaps even more so in a virtual one. Establishing these conditions begins from the first interactions students have with the teacher. We know that

- Strong teacher–student relationships rely on effective communication and a willingness to address issues that strain the relationship.

- Positive relationships are fostered and maintained when teachers set fair expectations, involve students in determining aspects of the classroom organization and management, and hold students accountable for the expectations in an equitable way.

- Importantly, relationships are not destroyed when problematic behaviors occur, either on the part of the teacher or students. This is an important point for educators. If we want to ensure students read, write, communicate, and think at high levels, we have to develop positive, trusting relationships with *each* student.

As important, high levels of positive relationships build trust and make the classroom a safe place to explore what students do not know, their errors and misconceptions. Indeed powerful student–teacher relationships allow errors to be seen as opportunities to learn. A lot of students (and teachers) avoid situations where they are likely to make errors, feel challenged with exposing their lack of knowledge or understanding, but we want to turn these situations into powerful learning opportunities, and this is more likely to occur in high trust environments. And it is not just high positive levels of teacher–student relations, but how you develop high trust student–student relations so one student can talk about their struggles of learning with other students, and the notion of "struggle" becomes a positive and fun activity.

When students struggle and do not achieve well, the relationship with the teacher usually suffers. When students are not achieving well, there is evidence that teachers treat them differently, thus further damaging the relationship. A study of differential teacher treatment of students found that low-achieving students (Good, 1987)

- Are criticized more often for failure

- Are praised less frequently

- Receive less feedback

- Are called on less often

- Have less eye contact from the teacher

- Have fewer friendly interactions with the teacher

- Experience acceptance of their ideas less often

Each of these can just as easily occur in a virtual classroom. There is another term for this: a "chilly" classroom climate in which some students do not feel they are valued and instead feel that "their presence . . . is at best peripheral, and at worst an unwelcome intrusion" (Hall & Sandler, 1982, p. 3). We do not in any way believe that these differential teacher behaviors are conscious and intentional. One speculation is that because educators don't feel successful with students they view as lower achieving, we subconsciously avoid contact with them. After all, we were human beings long before we became educators, and as social animals we attempt to surround ourselves with people who make us feel good about ourselves. Students who are not making gains make us feel like failures, and so we detach ourselves even more.

Now view Good's list from the opposite direction—students we see as being high achieving get more of us. Our attention, our contact, our interactions are more frequent, sustained, and growth producing. It is understandable that we gravitate to those students that make us feel successful as educators. But it is also a version of the Matthew effect, this time in attention rather than reading—the rich get richer while the poor get poorer (Stanovich, 1986). In this case, it's our positive attention that is gold.

MAKE IT ACTIONABLE

Imagine flipping the switch on this narrative by intentionally increasing the positive attention students who are perceived as lower performing receive. We don't mean suddenly focusing all attention on the three students that fall into that category while neglecting all the others. A quick pivot like that might be viewed as alarming or dismaying. However, waging a thoughtful campaign to change the dynamic is likely to have another benefit. Those students are likely to grow on the teacher and will probably learn more as a result. We'll borrow advice attributed to Archbishop Desmond Tutu that sometimes you have to "act your way into being." In other words, sometimes the change in behavior precedes the change in perception.

Identify three students who are not achieving well in the class. During live interactions, keep a tally of the following teacher-initiated behaviors. Or even better, have the teacher keep track and talk with you about the analysis.

SOMETIMES YOU HAVE TO "ACT YOUR WAY INTO BEING."

Interaction	Student 1	Student 2	Student 3
Did the teacher greet the student by name when they entered the virtual classroom?			
How many times did the teacher use the student's name (not as a correction) during the session?			
Did the teacher ask the student a critical thinking question related to the content?			
Did the teacher ask the student a personal question?			
Did the teacher pay the student a compliment?			
How many times did the teacher provide the student with praise for learning performance?			

LEADERSHIP

After you have collected data across several sessions, examine it and make some decisions about what you want to address. Ask yourself, how I can support the teacher to develop stronger relationships with these students and increase the expectations this teacher has for these students?

ENSURE CULTURALLY SUSTAINING PEDAGOGIES

ESSENTIAL QUESTION: How can distance learning be utilized to ensure a student-centered learning climate?

YOUR GOAL: Examine curriculum and instruction for evidence of culturally sustaining pedagogies.

Culturally sustaining pedagogies (CSP) are an approach to teaching and learning designed to move marginalized youth to the center, and in doing so to shift from a deficit-based to assets-based education. CSP is the product of the instructional and curricular choices a school makes and lies at the heart of equity work. Perhaps Brown (2019) says it most succinctly: Culturally sustaining pedagogies "ask educators to see young people as 'whole versus broken' when they enter our classrooms" (p. 43). The enduring question in CSP that cuts across all subject matter is this: *How do our students learn about themselves and the world?* Curriculum and instruction are marshalled to help students continually answer that question through the use of materials and pedagogy that deepen their knowledge and encourage them to find their voice.

CSP requires that we see ourselves as strengths-spotters. We use those assets that students bring to their benefit. This represents a shift for teachers who exhibit deficit thinking and focus on identifying what students don't know rather than leveraging what they do know. This is a true danger right now as months of interrupted schooling are prompting discussions about remediation due to the "COVID slide." It is hard to imagine that what we teach and how we teach it will remain untouched by events of 2020, including a global pandemic, racial injustices, and exposure of systemic inequities. A stance toward CSP recognizes that the past and the present merge and diverge, and that it is essential for learners to develop ways to critically interact with knowledge in order to create new knowledge from it (Paris & Alim, 2017).

The assets that students bring, and that families and communities offer, is key to accelerating their learning. The communication and language that students bring to the digital learning environment are equally important. Culturally proficient digital spaces honor multiple World Englishes as well as the heritage languages of students. The texts that are used are culturally and ethnically relevant. Popular culture is used to link contemporary issues to historical ones beyond the dominant culture. The language that teachers use is actively antiracist and the impact of racial bias is discussed in the context of both personal experiences and historical traumas.

It is vital to note that the importance of CSP is not limited to schools that serve students of color. All students need to learn about the lives and experiences of others.

In fact, it is all the more important to teach about those not directly represented, including Black, Latinx, and indigenous people. To fail to do so is to narrow knowledge and to continue to foster silos of isolation that perpetuate inequities.

Nor is an assets-based approach restricted to students. People of color on your staff are assets to the school. Educators of color leave the profession at disproportionately higher rates. Their reasons for leaving focus primarily on the workplace environment, including experiencing an antagonistic school climate, feeling undervalued, and reduced agency and autonomy (Education Trust, 2019). As a school leader, the creation of a culturally sustaining school climate includes empowering teachers to use culturally sustaining instructional practices to build relevancy. "Affirming the humanity and identity . . . by ensuring curriculum, learning, and work environments are inclusive and respectful of all racial ethnic groups" benefits students, teachers, and the community (Education Trust, 2019, p. 27).

MAKE IT ACTIONABLE

High-quality education in distance learning demands even more from us in terms of student engagement for learning. We simply will not get the results we want without pivoting our focus to educational relevancy in the eyes of students. Questions about a culturally sustaining pedagogy using an assets-based approach are not easily addressed in a checklist. Rather, these questions persist across the school year and are used regularly to improve our practices. We have found that the questions posed by Muhammed (2019) are useful for propelling discussion and action.

NOTE TO SELF

As you meet with teachers about curriculum and instruction in distance learning, pose these questions for discussion. What evidence are you discovering? Where are their opportunities for growth?

	REFLECTIVE QUESTIONS FOR SCHOOLS
Skill	How does our instruction and text selection build students' skills and standards?
Intellect	How does our instruction and text selection build students' knowledge and mental powers?
Identity	How does our instruction and text selection help students learn something about themselves and about others?
Criticality	How does our instruction and text selection engage students' thinking about power, equity, and the disruption of oppression?

Source: Adapted from Muhammad, G. (2019). Protest, power, and possibilities: The need for agitation literacies. *Journal of Adolescent & Adult Literacy, 63*(3), 353. Used with permission.

USE A DISTANCE LEARNING INSTRUCTIONAL FRAMEWORK

ESSENTIAL QUESTION: How do I articulate effective instruction in a distance learning environment?

YOUR GOAL: Use an instructional framework designed with distance learning in mind to hone your instructional leadership skills.

Effective school leaders recognize when sound instructional principles are enacted in a physical classroom. The structure of the day is time bound, and important stages of learning are fostered in real time. For example, there is a set time scheduled for a literacy block or a science class, and teaching is conducted within this dimension. But in distance learning, teachers must consider the various ways and times that students will access the class. Synchronous and asynchronous learning opportunities are spread across a week and in doses that may vary a bit from one day to the next. Teachers are making decisions about what learning experiences might be best suited for these virtual environments, and likely struggle with how to do so.

As an instructional leader, you communicate, observe, and guide teachers, and teaching at a distance raises different challenges. With live virtual sessions of

Figure 3.1 Instructional Framework

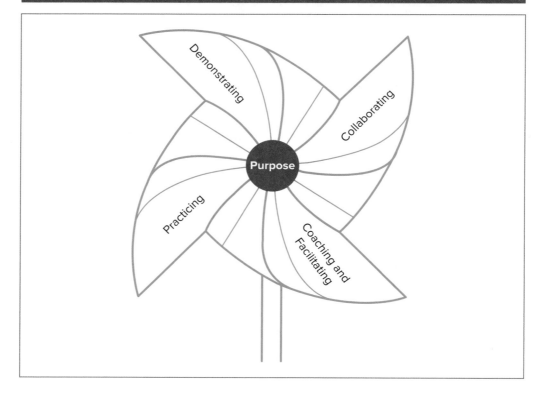

much shorter duration than the school day, what occurs in them is a priority. Asynchronous learning has taken on new importance, but it can't be endless electronic worksheets. Build common vocabulary so that distance learning teachers can collaborate to design instruction.

1. **Demonstrating:** *What input do students need from teachers*? Direct instruction, modeling, and worked examples are important, but might be recorded and posted for asynchronous learning in advance of, or after, live virtual sessions.

2. **Collaborating:** *How will students learn from each other? How will the teacher hold students accountable for their collaborative learning?* Meaningful peer interaction is essential and may take place in live sessions and during asynchronous small group tasks.

3. **Coaching and facilitating:** *How will students receive scaffolded instruction?* Guided learning and immediate feedback are a centerpiece of learning and have a prime role in live sessions.

4. **Practicing:** *How will students practice and apply what they have learned?* Practice should be deliberate and spaced to ensure long-term learning. Asynchronous tasks should build on initial instruction and foster transfer of learning.

MAKE IT ACTIONABLE

Develop your own observation skills by visiting live sessions and teachers' learning management systems to gain a better sense of synchronous and asynchronous learning at your school. Talk with teachers about how they are addressing each of these phases of learning. Learn about emerging practices in your school so that you can leverage them and identify potential gaps to support teachers' instructional skills. In the sections that follow, we will explore each in more detail and suggest look-fors as you observe and coach.

LEADERSHIP

NOTE TO SELF

Consider the following questions as you visit virtual classrooms. Be sure you are looking at both the synchronous and asynchronous elements of learning to hone your skills.

1. How is the purpose of learning being communicated?

2. How are students acquiring new knowledge, concepts, or skills?

3. How are collaborative tasks occurring?

4. In what ways is student thinking being facilitated and coached?

5. How is practice being leveraged so that students can apply what they have learned?

DEMONSTRATING IN DISTANCE LEARNING

Demonstrations provide students with explicit instruction of what they will do or learn. There are a number of ways that teachers can demonstrate skills and concepts for students, including direct instruction and think-alouds and think-alongs. However, a challenge in distance learning has to do with the time allotted. In physical classrooms, the evidence is that teachers fill the air with the vast majority of their own talk and vastly underestimate how much they talk. Having said that, teachers do need to devote some time providing explicit instruction in clear and concise ways. The tension distance learning produces is that the amount of time we get with students for live instruction is less compared to what we have come to expect in a brick-and-mortar classroom. Live sessions simply cannot be filled with long lectures while students sit passively staring at their screens. The answer is to create tight and precise demonstrations that are infused with expert thinking while also conserving time such that collaboration and coaching can take place.

> **ESSENTIAL QUESTION:** How can teachers capitalize on effective practices when demonstrating skills or concepts?
>
> **YOUR GOAL:** Coach and support teachers in their efforts to provide robust direct instruction and modeled thinking.

Direct instruction. Direct instruction is means for demonstrating concepts or skills for students. To be sure, direct instruction has gotten a bad rap in some quarters. In fact, it might be one of the most misunderstood instructional approaches out there. False impressions about direct instruction usually cluster into three categories:

1. It is scripted and didactic.
2. It is inflexible.
3. It devalues teacher judgment.

However, these misconceptions prevent people from implementing something that can work. With an effect size of 0.59, direct instruction offers a pedagogical pathway that provides students with the modeling, scaffolding, and practice they require when learning new skills and concepts. Rosenshine (2008) noted that the structure of a direct instruction lesson should follow a pattern that includes the following:

1. Start the lesson with a short statement of goals.
2. Provide a short review of previous learning. Going from the known to the new is powerful.
3. Present new material in small steps, providing practice for students after each step.
4. Give clear and detailed instructions and explanations.

LEADERSHIP

5. Provide a high level of active practice for all students.

6. Ask questions, check for student understanding, and obtain responses from all students.

7. Provide explicit instruction and guide students during initial practice.

Think-alongs. Thinking is invisible. A major aim with this demonstration technique is to help make this thinking more visible. Sharing thinking with students allows them a glimpse into the inner workings of our brains as we process and act upon information. The research world calls this a *think-aloud* but we worry that this term focuses exclusively on the teacher, so we like to use the phrase "think-along" to ensure that students are engaged in the process as their teachers think-aloud.

Our experience has been that off-the-cuff think-alongs tend to be unfocused and can leave students more confused. A planned think-along ensures a higher degree of clarity. Resist the urge to clutter your think-alongs with too many divergent ideas—it shouldn't be a stream of consciousness.

Think-alongs, as with most other forms of demonstrating, are delivered using first-person language. This spoken language mirrors one's own internal dialogue. These "I" statements can feel awkward at first, but they contribute to a think-along's effectiveness by triggering empathetic listening on the part of the student. It is human nature to respond emotionally to such statements. The use of "I" statements invites students into the thinking process in ways that second-person directives do not. Consider the difference between the two:

- **First-person statement:** "When I read this term, I'm confused so I scan back up to the bolded definition in the previous paragraph to remind myself what it means."

- **Second-person statement:** "When you run into an unfamiliar term, remember to scan back up and reread the bolded definition."

The first example gives students insight into the use of a comprehension strategy as it is deployed during the act of reading. The second, while good advice, uncouples the strategy from the decision to use it. Novice learners don't just need to know what the strategy is—they need to know when to apply it.

MAKE IT ACTIONABLE

The purpose of look-fors is to give you a starting point for learning more about how instructional moves occur in virtual spaces. These look-fors should not be used for the purpose of teacher evaluation, nor should it be expected that every one of these look-fors is present in a given lesson. By developing a skilled eye for understanding instructional moves during distance learning, you are better able to coach, provide support, and deploy resources for professional learning.

Hone your coaching skills as an instructional leader by observing demonstration lessons in synchronous or asynchronous environments. Use the list of look-fors as you observe and learn.

Pacing	• The time allotted for demonstration is developmentally appropriate.
	• The demonstration is concise and makes efficient use of time.
	• The pace of the lesson is steady and consistent.
Rigor and Alignment	• The demonstration is grade appropriate and aligned with standards or expectations for learning.
Statement of Goals	• The demonstration includes a statement of the goal for the lesson.
	• The teacher names the skill, concept, or strategy being demonstrated.
Explanations and Examples	• Explanations are clear and developmentally appropriate.
	• Examples and non-examples illuminate the skill or concept being taught.
Modeling	• The demonstration includes modeling of the skill or concept and the decisions made to use it.

COLLABORATING IN DISTANCE LEARNING

One of the teacher mindframes we value is "I engage as much in dialogue as in monologue." Peer collaboration and discussion is a linchpin of student learning. With an effect size of 0.82, student discussion has the potential to speed student learning (Hattie, 2020). Yet even in physical classrooms, student discussion is rare. Unfortunately, there are many classrooms in which teachers do almost all of the talking. One of the risks with distance learning is that teachers replicate all of that talk online or even increase the amount of talk so that they can fill the space. One study noted that the average amount of discussion in middle and high school classes was less than one minute per class period (Nystrand & Gamoran, 1997). Another student of classroom discourse found that while teachers asked an average of 200 questions *per day*, each student posed only two question *per week* (Clinton & Dawson, 2018).

ESSENTIAL QUESTION: How can student engagement and peer-to-peer interaction be fostered in a virtual environment?

YOUR GOAL: Coach and support teachers in their efforts to foster engagement and peer collaboration.

LEADERSHIP

Student dialogue can be a challenge to foster in a virtual environment. Students may feel awkward speaking in a virtual environment, and teachers may struggle a bit more with how to get them talking about their learning. Using students' names frequently and asking questions of specific students can acclimate them to expectations about discussion during live sessions. Posing questions and asking students to respond in the chat can familiarize them with tools meant to promote communication.

While these approaches can ease students into communicating more often, the use of a set of collaboration routines can lift the level of meaningful collaboration to higher levels. These routines should be explicitly taught and utilized frequently so that they can be easily enacted. Once learned, these peer-to-peer collaborations should be paired with robust tasks that foster intellectual interdependence. In other words, a collaboration task that could be completed independently, with little input from other group members, is not especially useful. On the other hand, collaborative tasks that require students to use reasoning, pose questions of one another, and resolve problems are of high value.

Collaboration should be featured in synchronous sessions so that the teacher can witness student thinking in real time. Some districts allow for breakout rooms to be used so that small groups of students can collaborate on a task. In these cases, the teacher should be actively joining groups throughout the collaboration to observe, spark ideas, and redirect as needed. Other districts do not allow breakout rooms unless there is an adult present. The logistical complications of doing so might mean that small group collaboration in this mode is limited. However, keep in mind that peer collaboration can occur as a fishbowl. While one small group collaborates, the other students and the teacher observe the process, ask questions, and make connections. As one example, a virtual version of a two-part collaboration might include a small group working through a task together, followed by a shift to the students who viewed the fishbowl now taking center stage to make connections, summarize, and extend.

MAKE IT ACTIONABLE

As noted previously, these look-fors are not for evaluative purposes. Rather, we have created them to support your learning as you engage with teachers in distance learning. Remember to involve your instructional leadership team, too, so that all of you can profit from the collective wisdom of the group.

NOTE TO SELF

Hone your coaching skills as an instructional leader by observing student collaboration and discussion in synchronous environments. Use the list of look-fors as you observe and learn.

Discussion	• Students have opportunities to engage in discussion in the live session.
	• The discussion is aligned with the academic learning in the session.
Routines	• The collaboration routine is familiar to students. If the routine is newer to students, it is accompanied with explicit instruction and modeling of the routine.
	• The collaboration routine used is developmentally appropriate.
Monitoring	• Student thinking is observed and monitored by the teacher.
	• The teacher provides affirmations and redirection when needed.
	• The teacher and students provide feedback to one another about the collaboration.
Task Design	• The task or problem is designed to promote intellectual interdependence.
	• The task is designed so that students use interpersonal skills and communication to successfully collaborate.
Links to Learning	• Students set goals before a collaborative task and monitor their success after the task.
	• Students are asked to draw conclusions and make connections to new or prior knowledge.

COACHING AND FACILITATING IN DISTANCE LEARNING

Small group learning allows teachers to meet individual needs, accelerate learning, and address misconceptions. This aspect of distance learning is one of the primary ways that teachers can support students. Essentially, this aspect of the learning focuses on supporting students' thinking while avoiding the temptation to tell them what to think. This requires that the teacher asks the right question to get the student to do the thinking. Importantly, appropriate scaffolding has an effect size of 0.58. When teachers are able to provide a range of scaffolds, students learn more.

ESSENTIAL QUESTION: How can student learning be facilitated using scaffolded instruction in a virtual environment?

YOUR GOAL: Coach and support teachers in their efforts to provide responsive small-group instruction.

When coaching and facilitating, students are taking on the cognitive load using what Vygotsky called the zone of proximal development. The learner is doing something challenging—something he wouldn't be able to do independently or with minimal guidance. This is exactly the time when the rigor is increased so that the students involved can stretch beyond their present level of performance. Therefore, coaching and facilitating sessions are about students applying learning in new situations.

Because of the responsive nature of this type of instruction, coaching and facilitating is typically conducted in live sessions. Given the scheduling required in advance, teachers can find themselves even more time bound in a distance learning setting. Unlike in a face-to-face classroom where the teacher may be able to extend the time just a bit longer with a small group, the stacked nature of back-to-back small-group sessions may prove challenging to do so. Of course, teachers can use breakout rooms to support their rapid transitions between groups. Be sure to check in with teachers to see if they are having scheduling challenges.

Students are often placed in a small group because they have a similar learning target. As with other aspects of instruction, the goals of the lesson should be shared so that students can monitor their learning. Whether it is for the purposes of deepening a new skill or concept, or extending learning, the grouping utilized should be flexible and done with intention. In all cases, the content of the lesson should stretch students a bit by providing them with a challenging, put not impossible task. After all, the teacher is there to bridge their learning as needed. This bridging effect is accomplished using scaffolds that rely on prompts and cues (Frey & Fisher, 2010).

When a student stalls, teachers begin by offering a prompt that sparks thinking. In some cases, this may be one that activates their prior knowledge (e.g., "What do you remember about the states of matter?") or reminds them of a procedure or process they temporarily forgot to apply (e.g., "Think about which problem-solving strategies we have used that might get you started."). The prompt might also be meant to cause reflection on the metacognition, such as saying, "I see you're thinking strategically. What would be the next logical step?"

There are times when a prompt or two isn't sufficient to get the student moving forward. That's when cues are helpful. Cues shift the student's attention more overtly. They might include a gesture paired with a verbal response (e.g., "Can you see the part of the diagram I'm pointing to with the annotation tool? How could that information help you right now?") or reminding them to reread a specific paragraph to locate the information they need.

MAKE IT ACTIONABLE

Because of the responsive nature of coaching and facilitation sessions, it is very likely that not all of these look-fors will be present. Follow up these sessions with questions to the teacher about the decisions made during the lesson. It is of great value to gain insight into how teachers notice and respond to student learning in the moment.

PRACTICING IN DISTANCE LEARNING

There are several takeaways from the crisis teaching that occurred in the spring of 2020. The first was that educators around the globe pulled off the unimaginable. Through heroic efforts on the part of leaders, teachers, support staff, and clerical workers, children experienced some form of learning for nine weeks. With little more than a weekend to prepare, schooling shifted to an online environment. We used what we had at our disposal, which included hastily prepared worksheet packets. Most of these would not have been used had physical schooling continued. However, we scrambled to find almost anything that would be somewhat school-like.

ESSENTIAL QUESTION: How can deliberate practice be implemented in a virtual environment?

YOUR GOAL: Coach and support teachers in their efforts to provide targeted practice work in asynchronous learning that is designed to extend skills.

The second takeaway was that the practice work assigned during that time was often less than ideal. With little opportunity to make decisions about precisely what students needed to practice, some students practiced things they already knew well, meaning that it was nothing more than busy work. Other students attempted to practice things that were well beyond their reach. An ongoing challenge is that practice is essential to learning, but it needs to be the right practice at the right time. In face-to-face classrooms, teachers were able to oversee practice work more directly (although it wasn't always the right work, even then). In asynchronous distance learning, we are witnessing a gap in the habits and dispositions that students require in order to engage in practice such that it yields results for them. We need to teach students the whys and the hows of practice and pair that approach with work that encourages rehearsal and retrieval of information.

One of the findings related to practice in the Visible Learning database is that *spaced practice* is much more effective than *mass practice*. In fact, the effect size of spaced practice is 0.65. The implications for distance learning (not to mention face-to-face classes) is that students should cycle through practice experiences across time. Rather than assign fifteen odd-numbered problems on a given day, space them out. And include problems from the past so that students still have to apply their knowledge to those types of challenges. It's better to have students practice thirty minutes each day rather than 2.5 hours on Friday.

In addition, *deliberate practice* is important. The effect size is 0.79. We recognize that "practice" is often equated with "mindless repetitions," which is counter to deliberate practice. To get the effect size of 0.79, students must focus their attention and engage in the tasks with the specific goal of improving performance, and there needs to be feedback that helps students know where best to move next in their learning. Goals are crucial in practice, just as they are in every other aspect of learning. Practice work that is distributed across the week and that includes student self-assessment and goal-setting increases the likelihood that the learning will stick. And practice is the cement that holds learning together. Without practice, the learning designed to occur during the demonstrating, collaborating, coaching, and facilitating phases is diminished. High quality practice, not mindless compliance tasks, is what speeds the pace of learning.

Imagine wanting to learn to play the piano. Both instruction and practice are important. As the learner, you need to know what it looks like, sounds like, and feels like to play the piano. That comes from instruction. But then, you practice and seek feedback as you begin to approximate the playing that has been modeled for you.

HIGH QUALITY PRACTICE, NOT MINDLESS COMPLIANCE TASKS, IS WHAT SPEEDS THE PACE OF LEARNING.

MAKE IT ACTIONABLE

It's difficult to observe practice in real time, as this dimension of learning primarily occurs asynchronously. Talk with teachers about the decisions they make as they design practice. Check in with a student focus group about their knowledge, habits, and dispositions toward practice. These listen-fors can be invaluable for informing professional learning and directing resources.

NOTE TO SELF

Use these listen-fors as a guide when you talk with teachers and students about the role of practice and its implementation in distance learning. Use what you have learned to collaborate with your instructional leadership team about next steps to strengthen the distance learning program.

Teacher Knowledge and Decision Making on Practice	• Students have been taught about the role of practice in their learning. • The practice work is based on student learning data, including student feedback. • Practice work includes opportunities for students to set goals and self-assess.
Teacher Habits and Dispositions About Practice	• Submitted practice work is accompanied by timely teacher feedback, usually within one week. • Student performance on practice work is used to inform future instruction. • A student who struggles to complete practice work is not labeled as "unmotivated" but rather receives additional support to build practice habits.
Student Knowledge About Practice	• Students know about the role of practice in their learning. • They view practice as being more than just a form of compliance. • Students know about the benefits of spaced and deliberate practice.
Student Habits and Dispositions About Practice	• Students set practice goals for themselves. • Students engage in self-assessments that narrow their focus on what needs to be practiced.

LEADERSHIP

4 MINDFRAMES FOR LEADERS FROM A DISTANCE

How you think about your work has an impact on the way you do the work and the decisions you make. We have saved this section for last as we believe that the following mindframes will serve you well, long after the current crises has passed. In fact, during distance learning you have an opportunity to practice and develop these mindframes. We encourage you to take some time to think about your internal operating system, or mindframes, and how these might help you lead from a distance and into the future.

In this section:

- ☐ I AM AN EVALUATOR OF MY IMPACT ON TEACHER AND STUDENT LEARNING.
- ☐ I SEE ASSESSMENT AS INFORMING MY IMPACT AND NEXT STEPS.
- ☐ I COLLABORATE WITH MY PEERS AND MY TEACHERS ABOUT MY CONCEPTIONS OF PROGRESS AND MY IMPACT.
- ☐ I AM A CHANGE AGENT AND I BELIEVE ALL TEACHERS AND STUDENTS CAN IMPROVE.
- ☐ I STRIVE FOR CHALLENGE RATHER THAN MERELY DOING MY BEST.
- ☐ I GIVE AND HELP STUDENTS AND TEACHERS UNDERSTAND FEEDBACK AND I INTERPRET AND ACT ON FEEDBACK GIVEN TO ME.
- ☐ I ENGAGE AS MUCH IN DIALOGUE AS IN MONOLOGUE.
- ☐ I EXPLICITLY INFORM TEACHERS AND STUDENTS WHAT SUCCESSFUL IMPACT LOOKS LIKE FROM THE OUTSET.
- ☐ I BUILD RELATIONSHIPS AND TRUST SO THAT LEARNING CAN OCCUR IN A PLACE WHERE IT IS SAFE TO MAKE MISTAKES AND LEARN FROM OTHERS.
- ☐ I FOCUS ON LEARNING AND THE LANGUAGE OF LEARNING.

"We've got this!" That's how principal Jesse Salcedo starts and ends each session with teachers and staff. As he says, "We have to focus on the things that are in our control and lead with confidence. I want the people I work with to feel the confidence, even if I don't have all of the answers. I want people to know that we are working hard to ensure that they are supported and that their students continue to learn. It's actually my choice, how I choose to view the world. I choose positive. It's my mindset that makes the difference."

We agree with Mr. Salcedo. The underlying beliefs that you have will influence the decisions you make and the way that you interact with others. The Visible Learning research calls them mindframes and they are the mental attitudes and habits important for leadership. We have saved the leadership mindframes for last because we recognize that there are many logistics that must be addressed in leading from a distance. But even more importantly, we hope that these mindframes endure long after distance learning. In fact, we hope these mindframes guide your efforts to bring schools back even better than they were before. In this section, we present ten mindframes for leaders, which were first introduced by Hattie and Smith (2021) but we have adapted for distance learning. Each mindframe is a principle that serves you well, irrespective of the format of schooling. The following mindframes focus on self-regulation—or the ability to control and direct one's behavior, emotions, and thoughts:

1. I am an evaluator of my impact on teacher and student learning.

2. I see assessment as informing my impact and next steps.

3. I collaborate with my peers and my teachers about my conceptions of progress and my impact.

4. I am a change agent and I believe all teachers and students can improve.

5. I strive for challenge rather than merely doing my best.

6. I give and help students and teachers understand feedback and I interpret and act on feedback given to me.

7. I engage as much in dialogue as in monologue.

8. I explicitly inform teachers and students what successful impact looks like from the outset.

9. I build relationships and trust so that learning can occur in a place where it is safe to make mistakes and learn from others.

10. I focus on learning and the language of learning.

What are your initial thoughts as you read that list? Did you recognize yourself in some or many? Are you interested in how developing these mindsets can serve you well as you lead your school or system from a distance? Before you move into this section of the playbook, take a few minutes to self-assess where you currently are in building a virtual school climate.

DRAWING ON MY EXPERTISE

Think about the current context of your school during distance learning. Use the traffic light scale to reflect on your practices as a school leader. To what extent is each of these statements true?

Scale	Statement
●————————●	1. I am an evaluator of my impact on teacher and student learning.
●————————●	2. I see assessment as informing my impact and next steps.
●————————●	3. I collaborate with my peers and my teachers about my conceptions of progress and my impact.
●————————●	4. I am a change agent and I believe all teachers and students can improve.
●————————●	5. I strive for challenge rather than merely doing my best.
●————————●	6. I give and help students and teachers understand feedback and I interpret and act on feedback given to me.
●————————●	7. I engage as much in dialogue as in monologue.
●————————●	8. I explicitly inform teachers and students what successful impact looks like from the outset.
●————————●	9. I build relationships and trust so that learning can occur in a place where it is safe to make mistakes and learn from others.
●————————●	10. I focus on learning and the language of learning.

MINDFRAME 1

I am an evaluator of my impact on teacher and student learning.

As we have noted earlier, the average impact from principals on student learning is 0.37, slightly below average. Like all averages, it hides the remarkable variance in the impact of school leaders because of their mindframes. Thus the question is, what are the mindframes of school leaders such that you can increase your

MINDFRAMES

impact? If you work to create a healthy climate, deliver on the promise of equity, serve as an instructional leader, and guide the professional learning of teachers, your impact should be significant. So a better question is, how do you know that you are having an impact? And what can you do if the impact is not where you want it?

One way to plan for the eventual assessment of your impact is to create a simple logic model. Logic models provide an overview of how your effort is supposed to work and describe what happens when the actions are accomplished (Julian, 1997). Others call this a theory of change or even a road map. Having a logic model allows you to identify a common challenge, allocate resources, project the impact, and then monitor it for success. There are a number of different tools that you can use. We've included a simple logic model that a leadership team developed to increase attendance in distance learning (see Figure 4.1). Attendance in synchronous sessions had decreased and teachers were concerned. As the principal noted, they had a challenge and knew the outcome they hoped for. Thinking evaluatively allowed the administrative team to determine their impact.

MAKE IT ACTIONABLE

The first step is to diagnose a common challenge. What is something that is impeding the learning of teachers or students? You may have a few logic models operating at the same time. The goal is to determine if they are effective and having the desired impact. To engage in diagnosis, develop logic models, and then implement them to ensure effectiveness and impact requires a particular way of thinking. Evaluative thinking is the core principle underpinning all of the mindframes for leaders. As Clinton (2021) noted, "evaluative thinking is a cognitive process; it's a way of being" (p. 14). It involves the proficiency to ask, "What is my impact?" and collect the evidence of your actions and leadership of teachers that will help to answer this evaluative question. Thus, as you think through the logic model, consider the ways in which you can ask questions, collect data, and take action.

From there, identify the resources and activities that are likely to be useful and identify the outputs and outcomes. This is not a solo activity; use your leadership team. But remember this mindframe is about developing a type of thinking: that of an evaluator who looks at data, is skilled in interpretation and storytelling based on these data, and makes decisions based on what the data say. And it's about reflecting on the impact that you had on both teachers and students.

Figure 4.1 Goal: Increase attendance in synchronous distance learning sessions.

Our Intended Work		Our Intended Results	
Resources	**Activities**	**Outputs** *Direct Benefits*	**Outcomes** *Indirect Benefits*
*If we have access to these resources, **then** these activities can be completed.*			
	*If we successfully complete these activities, **then** these changes will occur as a direct result of the actions.*		
		*If the activities are carried out as designed, **then** these changes will result.*	
			*If participants benefit from our efforts, **then** other systems, organizations, or communities will change.*
• Leadership team comprising key stakeholders • Communication systems with families • Articulated expectations for attendance • Attendance team • Counseling supports in place • Record-keeping procedures and alert systems • Training materials	• Attendance recorded by teachers within ten minutes of class starting • Daily attendance review at 10 AM • Attendance team making personal calls • School leadership contacts family when there is a failure to connect • Information sessions for students and families on the impact of learning days missed • Incentives for positive attendance • Reengagement plan including a socially distanced home visit for any student who misses two days or more in a week • Activation of counseling services as needed • Provide ongoing training on best practices	• Increased attendance (online) of students and staff in distance learning events • Increased educational attainment • Increased social and emotional competence among students • Increased satisfaction of parents	• Improved school climate • Improved mental and physical health outcomes • Improved job satisfaction for staff • Improved social capital of the community

NOTE TO SELF

Use the template for a logic model to develop a plan that will allow you to determine your impact.

OUR INTENDED WORK		OUR INTENDED RESULTS	
RESOURCES	**ACTIVITIES**	**OUTPUTS** *DIRECT* **BENEFITS**	**OUTCOMES** *INDIRECT* **BENEFITS**
*If we have access to these resources, **then** these activities can be completed.*			
	*If we successfully complete these activities, **then** these changes will occur as a direct result of the actions.*		
		*If the activities are carried out as designed, **then** these changes will result.*	
			*If participants benefit from our efforts, **then** other systems, organizations, or communities will change.*

MINDFRAME 2

I see assessment as informing my impact and next steps.

Schools are awash with information. But most of it is not used to determine the impact that teachers and leaders have on students. Imagine if we used the available data to determine our impact and then planned next steps for personal and school improvement. It's much like we recommend to teachers. It's about interpretation, shared interpretation, and action based on these interpretations. Use the interpretation of the data you have around you to make decisions about your impact and how you can move student learning forward.

ESSENTIAL QUESTION: What data do you access to note your impact?

YOUR GOAL: Use assessment information wisely.

The students at DuPaul Middle School were not performing well on their end-of-unit assessments. As the principal noted, it was pretty much across the board. The attendance and participation rates, reported in the data, were respectable. In fact, they were better than many of the schools in the district. But the assessment results, and thus grade point averages, were far below those from the previous year and at least half of the other middle schools in the district. These data are begging for defensible interpretations. The team combed through the data and could not reasonably determine why the scores were so low. Then they visited synchronous sessions, talked with teachers, and reviewed assignments in the learning management system.

And there it was. The tasks that were being assigned were not aligned with grade-level expectations, but the assessments were. In fact, the assessments had been developed during previous school years. But the tasks were less rigorous than the assessments. This is not uncommon as others have documented the fact that assignments are often not aligned with grade-level expectations (TNTP, 2018). In their discussion with teachers, the leaders noted that the teachers were well intentioned and wanted to ensure that students were successful in distance learning. This tension—between ensuring students experienced success in a new learning environment and expecting students to achieve—was the source of the challenge. And the leaders had to engage in dialogue with teachers to better understand the next steps and to ensure that students learned what they were supposed to.

MINDFRAMES

NOTE TO SELF

Use these questions to reach decisions about conceptual and procedural issues for gathering data. You should not feel restricted to the choices listed here.

What is our purpose for gathering this data?	• To aid in planning for the future • To identify an opportunity to improve learning • To get feedback from students • To find out about a nonacademic or social and emotional learning indicator • Other
What is the scope of the data collection?	• Entire class or grade level • Representative sample • Targeted students
What are the characteristics of the time frame when the data will be collected?	• Specific date, week, or month • Periodically, until improvement is seen
What data source(s) will help us answer our question about current levels of student performance?	• Student work samples • Performance data results (standards based) • Performance data results (classroom based) • Attendance data • Participation rates • Survey • Interview • Other

Depending on the results of your team time discussions, you are likely to need additional time for gathering the data. If the data needed are not immediately available, develop a list of tasks so that the data will be made available for the next meeting. Be sure to charge specific team members with gathering the data the team members agreed they needed.

Data Needed	Who Will Gather It	Date Needed
Preparing for the Data Analysis Protocol *How will the data be assembled and shared with the team?*		

MAKE IT ACTIONABLE

Once you and your team have a sufficient amount of data, the next step requires an analysis of the data to determine potential steps moving forward. A protocol can serve as a powerful resource in keeping the team focused and efficient during data analysis. It is easy and tempting at times to digress into topics that are not going to impact student growth and achievement. Using a protocol is a way to avoid these diversions while maintaining a structure that supports the intended purpose of the analysis. Take a moment to review the following protocol, which is adapted from the National School Reform Faculty.

MINDFRAMES

Protocol for Examining Data

Purpose: This protocol is for use in guiding a group through analysis of data to identify strengths and common challenges.

Materials: Copies of data for team members, highlighters, chart paper, note-taking guide on next page.

Checklist to Support Activation

____ Multiple forms of data are used

____ Evidence and research inform decisions

Sample Questions to Support Activation

- How have we used multiple forms of data today to drive our decisions?

- What evidence-based research impacted our decision making?

- What might be other factors that could be impacting the data?

- How do these data affirm what we currently think?

- How do these data disrupt what we currently think and why?

Sample Sentence Starters to Support Activation

- These data are different from what I originally thought because _____.

- A possible cause of the data is _____.

- An evidence-based practice we can think about is _____.

Getting Started—Overview of Data (3 minutes)

A team member gives a brief description of the particular data to be discussed and answers clarifying questions as necessary.

Step 1: What parts of these data catch your attention? Just the facts (10 minutes): 2 minutes silently writing individual observations, 8 minutes discussing as a group.

Step 2: What do the data tell us? What does the data NOT tell us? (10 minutes): 3 minutes silently making notes, 7 minutes discussing as a group. Make inferences about the data. *The leader encourages team members to support their statements with evidence from the data.*

Step 3: What good news is there to celebrate? (5 minutes to identify strengths) *The leader asks the group to look for indications of success in the data.*

Step 4: What are possible common challenges suggested by the data? (10 minutes): 3 minutes silently writing individual ideas for practice, 7 minutes for group discussion. *The leader helps the group narrow the list of possible common challenges to no more than three.*

Step 5: What are our key conclusions? (5 minutes) In other words, what I and we do based on the data that have been collected.

This is a formal protocol that involves a team. As this mindframe develops, you will internalize this process and start to naturally use assessment information to help you determine your impact and your next steps.

MINDFRAME 3

I collaborate with my peers and my teachers about my conceptions of progress and my impact.

ESSENTIAL QUESTION: What is our collective leadership efficacy?

YOUR GOAL: Increase my team's belief in their ability to impact students' learning.

Collective teacher efficacy is the belief of a group that they possess as a team the wherewithal to positively impact student learning. Members of a group with a high degree of collective efficacy have confidence that they can successfully execute a course of action (Bandura, 1997). Evidence of collective efficacy transcends professions. Athletes draw on their beliefs about the success of their team to win the game. Military forces count on their beliefs that fellow soldiers are providing top-notch information and making wise decisions. In medicine, patients under the care of nurses with a high degree of collective efficacy heal more rapidly.

Collective teacher efficacy refers to a staff's shared belief that through their collective action, they can positively influence student outcomes, including those who are disengaged or disadvantaged. And it's powerful with an effect size of 1.39. In part, leaders need to foster and support teacher collective efficacy. Doing so requires that teams set goals, allocate resources such as time and effort, and collect evidence to determine their impact. It's an ongoing cycle that allows teams to see that their efforts are effective and, over time, they come to attribute success to their efforts. We noted the power of a professional learning cycle in the section on professional learning.

But this mindframe also notes the value of collaborating with peers. Donohoo (2021) notes that "collective leadership efficacy refers to principals' shared beliefs about their collective capacity to improve student outcomes within and across schools in the district" (p. 37). When leadership teams within the school and across the district believe that they will impact learning, set goals, allocate resources, collect evidence, and attribute their success to their efforts, the power of the collective is enhanced.

COLLECTIVE TEACHER EFFICACY: A STAFF'S SHARED BELIEF THAT THROUGH COLLECTIVE ACTION, THEY CAN POSITIVELY INFLUENCE STUDENT OUTCOMES.

Your reactions to these reflective statements are real. We don't want to discount or diminish your experiences and feelings. But if any of them are true for you, your ability to impact students' learning through collective efficacy will be compromised. And if your peers are engaged in the same reflective work, you might all just come to realize that we need to put some of our histories aside for the benefit of students.

MAKE IT ACTIONABLE

Distance learning has presented a number of challenges for teachers and some have even suggested that their belief in themselves has been compromised. As leaders with this mindframe, you want to ensure that your colleagues are motivated and supported.

Motivation comes, in part, when people see the task as relevant. Parenthetically, motivation also increases when people feel that they can be successful. The expectancy-value model of learning (Wigfield & Eccles, 2000) suggests that expectations regarding success and the value of completing a task affect an individual's behavior. Over time, cost was added to this model as individuals consider the return on their investment. There are many ways to use an expectancy-value-cost scale, including the value that people have for their collaboration with others or their engagement in distance learning. We have adapted the tool Kosovich, Hulleman, Barron, and Getty (2015) developed to determine students' motivation in math and science to learn. In our adaptation, this instrument can help you gauge teachers' motivation for continuous improvement of distance learning.

Item	Strongly Disagree (1)	Disagree (2)	Slightly Disagree (3)	Slightly Agree (4)	Agree (5)	Strongly Agree (6)
I know that I can learn to be an effective distance learning educator.						
I believe that I can be a success teaching at a distance.						
I think my class is important.						
I value my class and what it offers students.						
I think my class is useful for students.						
My preparation for distance learning classes takes too much time.						
Because of the other things that I do, I don't have time to put into my class.						
I am unable to put in the time needed to prepare well.						
I have to give up too much to teach from a distance well.						

This adapted survey has not been validated, but it has been used in a number of schools to provide leaders with data about teacher expectations, values, and costs. It helps leaders allocate their time and efforts to support teachers and maintain the collective efficacy of their teams. You could modify this tool and ask about the value, expectations, and costs of being part of team as well.

MINDFRAME 4

I am a change agent and I believe all teachers and students can improve.

Effective school leaders work together with others to effect change. The collective efficacy of any group is powered by trust and relationships. Efficacious groups seek out feedback and provide feedback to one another. Importantly, they resolve conflicts, make decisions and adapt based on their results. But the collective efficacy of a school staff is undermined

ESSENTIAL QUESTION: How can I serve as an agent of change and not simply try to change everything myself?

YOUR GOAL: Build the professional capital of others as you lead in distance learning.

when the school leader adopts a heroic stance (Robinson, Lloyd, & Rowe, 2008). Hardly anything will rob a group of its agency more quickly than having one person communicate that they alone are the Solver of All Problems. Instead of empowering colleagues to address challenges together, the hero-principal ushers in an era of learned helplessness. A global pandemic and the necessary shift to distance learning certainly counts as a change in need of lots of solutions. You simply cannot do it alone.

Building the agency of the group requires investing in the professional capital of the group (Hargreaves & Fullan, 2012). Professional capital refers to the human, social, and decisional capital of an organization. Social capital is a measure of the quality of the trusting relationships, while human capital is a measure of the professional skills of its members. The authors described the work of Leana (2011), an organizational management researcher, as an example of the effects of these two on student learning. She measured each in 130 schools and correlated them to mathematics achievement at the beginning and end of the school year. In other words, she wanted to gauge impact. Schools with high social capital (trusting collaborative relationships) did well. Schools with both high social capital and human capital (technical skills) did even better. Here's where it gets interesting. Students of teachers in schools that had high social capital but who themselves possessed low human capital did better, too. It turns out that when the conditions allow for staff to collaborate meaningfully with others, good teaching rubs off. In other words, you can build your human capital through social capital. However, the reverse is not true.

Decisional capital is the third factor. This is a measure of how one gains the ability to make judgments and decisions. Medical professionals, as one example, learn not just the technical skills needed, but they also acquire an increasing ability over their careers to make decisions about treatment. Educators must learn to do the same, both in the moment of active teaching (a practice referred to as noticing) and in planning future instruction. The ability to reflect, make decisions, and collaborate with others are all necessary for decisional capital to grow. Similarly, you can build human capital through decisional capital.

As a school leader your mindframe must be one that fosters the social and decisional capital of the organization. In terms of distance learning, we are all learning in real time. It is essential that emerging good practices are quickly disseminated. A major way to do so is ensure that teachers have opportunities to collaborate with one another. Just as importantly, staff must have an inclination to take up those emerging good practices. That's the trust factor. Your involvement is vital. You are a co-learner with them and you empower them to make decisions. You amplify what they are learning by feeding back to them to clarify ideas and decisions. Most importantly, you act upon those emerging solutions, helping to disseminate and support the uptake, and directing resources that support development. Fullan (2019, 2020) calls this "new leadership" and the timing couldn't be better. Figure 4.2 is a visual illustration of this model.

Figure 4.2 New Leadership

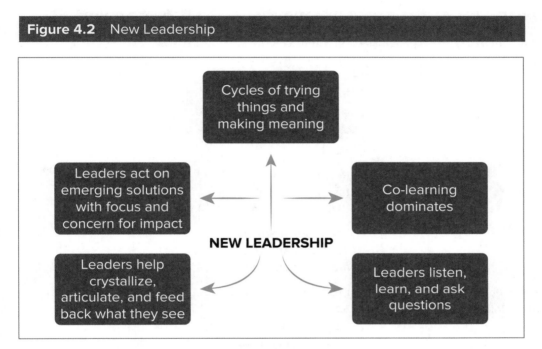

Source: Hattie, J., & Smith, R. (2020). *10 mindframes for leaders: The Visible Learning® approach to school success.* Thousand Oaks, CA: Corwin. Used with permission.

MAKE IT ACTIONABLE

As a change agent, you build the agency and collective efficacy of school teams. Access your current status as a school leader committed to building the professional capital of your organization in order to better address distance learning and speed the rate of change in adopting emerging wise practices.

Take inventory of current practices in place and areas of growth. These are key to the success of distance learning as schools rapidly learn and refine new practices. Identify growth opportunities for yourself and your school.

ELEMENT	ACTIONS	GROWTH OPPORTUNITIES
Investment in Social Capital	• Structures are in place for meaningful collaboration among teachers. • Time is allotted for collaboration to take place. • Relational trust is fostered through deliberate actions. • You listen, learn, and ask questions as a member of the group.	
Investment in Human Capital	• Professional learning about distance learning evolves through teacher input. • Professional learning aligned with student progress monitoring. • You are a co-learner with your staff.	
Investment in Decisional Capital	• Groups are empowered to make decisions. • You act on emerging solutions developed by the group.	

MINDFRAME 5

I strive for challenge rather than merely doing my best.

We have noted the value of goals in the instructional section of this book as well as the value of teams working on common challenges in this mindframes sections. Having goals is important. You should have instructional goals and you should have common challenges that are part of your logic model(s). But this mindframe is more personal. What goals do you have for yourself? How do you challenge yourself to be a better leader?

ESSENTIAL QUESTION: Do you believe that challenging yourself is valuable?

YOUR GOAL: I work to continue to improve as a leader.

Some people thrive on challenge; others avoid it. In fact, some people shrink away from challenge and just try to do their best. With all due respect, leaders must embrace challenges with confidence and support the members of their school community in doing so. None of us expected to be suddenly leading schools from a distance. But we are. It's a challenge. There have been challenges before and there will be challenges after this.

When you strive for challenge, you establish personal goals. And not just any goals. Your goal orientation is important. Goal orientation can be either mastery or performance. Martin (2013) explains, "Mastery orientation is focused on factors and processes such as effort, self-improvement, skill development, learning, and the task at hand. Performance orientation is focused more on demonstrating relative ability, social comparison, and outperforming others" (p. 353). In other words, it's the difference between saying, "I want to learn to speak Spanish" (mastery) rather than "I want to get an A in Spanish (performance)." Leaders tend to set both types of goals. They want their schools to be successful based on whatever measures are used in their systems. And they want to continually improve their leadership skills. Consider the following goals that some of the leaders who educated us about leading during distance learning set for themselves:

- Improve time management

- Develop emotional intelligence

- Strive to be antiracist

- Cultivate resilience

- Listen actively

- Improve public speaking skills

One of the tips from the world of business about setting personal, challenging goals is to focus on what you can control and then plan for the rest. That seems like good advice during a pandemic—or any other crisis.

NONE OF US EXPECTED TO BE SUDDENLY LEADING SCHOOLS FROM A DISTANCE. BUT WE ARE. IT'S A CHALLENGE. THERE HAVE BEEN CHALLENGES BEFORE AND THERE WILL BE CHALLENGES AFTER THIS.

MAKE IT ACTIONABLE

Stephen Goldberg of Optimus Performance recommends the KSS method. The *K* stands for keep doing, the *S* stands for stop doing, and the other *S* stands for start doing. By using this approach, you are recognizing what you do well, what you should no longer do and what you need to begin doing. They have developed a template that you can use to articulate your personal, challenge goal.

Goal Planning Sheet

Area	Today's Date	Final Target Date	Date Achieved

Goal (Specific, Measurable, Attainable, Realistic, Tangible)

_____

_____

_____

_____

Benefits From Achieving This Goal

_____

_____

_____

_____

Possible Obstacles

_____

_____

_____

_____

Possible Solutions

_____

_____

_____

_____

Specific Action Steps for Achieving This Goal	Responsible	Target Date	Date Completed
1.			
2.			
3.			
4.			
5.			
6.			
7.			
8.			
9.			
10.			
11.			
12.			

Method of Keeping Score _____

_____

Is it worth the time, effort and money to reach this goal?	Yes	No	Yes but later
Do I have the ability to achieve this goal?	Yes		No
Am I willing to do what it takes to achieve this goal?	Yes		No

Affirmations to Support This Goal

Source: Used with permission of Optimus Performance, optimusperfomance.ca

online resources ☐ Available for download at **resources.corwin.com/DLPlaybook-leaders**

MINDFRAMES

I give and help students and teachers understand feedback and I interpret and act on feedback given to me.

ESSENTIAL QUESTION: What role does feedback play in my leadership?

YOUR GOAL: Give, seek, and act upon feedback to improve learning outcomes for yourself, teachers, and students.

Feedback has the power to create change. But it doesn't always do so. It is important to note that the ultimate arbiter of the usefulness of feedback is the receiver, not the giver. It is the individual receiving the feedback who determines whether it is understandable, which means the giver must be attuned to feedback language. If an individual doesn't understand the feedback given, then it isn't useful. Period.

Further, perceptions about feedback are influenced by cultural and personal factors specific to the receiver, to be sure. However, a major factor is the relationship between the sender and receiver. If there is a weak relationship between the sender and receiver, the feedback is less likely to be received and used. When there is a strong relationship, the feedback is more likely to cause change.

Importantly, one of the best ways to ensure that feedback is received is to ensure that it's based on something that the receiver has asked for. There is a model of feedback called GREAT. The GREAT model developed by LarkApps, a team productivity and engagement company that specializes in supporting businesses whose employees work remotely but collaborate regularly. They note that building camaraderie at a distance is especially challenging, and that empathetic feedback is key to high performance. And don't we want the same thing for our students, whether face-to-face or in distance learning? The GREAT feedback framework consists of five facets:

- *Growth-oriented:* signal one's intention as constructive and focused on improvement
- *Real:* it's honest rather than that false praise as well as targeted, not holistic or vague
- *Empathetic:* combine criticism with care and a quest for understanding
- *Asked-for:* encourage the receiver to ask questions and seek feedback
- *Timely:* feedback gets stale fast, so you want to make sure it is delivered soon

Let's explore empathy a bit more. Given the realities that many students and teachers face during the pandemic, it's important to remain empathic while providing feedback. Empathetic feedback relies on micro-feedback and can be as simple as one thing to start, stop, or continue doing. Empathetic feedback is meant to be a dialogue, not a monologue. After providing the feedback, thank the receiver and ask questions that invite their input. After discussing their understanding, ask for feedback about your feedback. "Was this conversation helpful for you? Do you have advice for me about getting better at feedback?"

Finally, empathetic feedback shifts perspectives to ensure that the receiver benefits from your viewpoint while also seeing that you appreciate theirs. Once again, affective statements in the form of "I" messages are of value. Rather than voicing feedback in terms of "you" directives, affective statements frame the feedback as your own perspective. This allows psychological room for the student to listen and reduces that initial defensive clench that might otherwise shut down the conversation before it has begun. Empathetic feedback starters such as those in the Note to Self can set the stage for humane and growth-producing feedback.

NOTE TO SELF

INSTEAD OF	TRY
Can I give you some feedback?	Here's my reaction.
Good job!	Here are three things that really worked for me. What was going through your mind when you did them?
Here's what you should do.	Here's what I would do.
Here's where you need to improve.	Here's what worked best for me, and here's why.
That really didn't work.	When you did x, I felt y, or I didn't get that.
You need to improve your communication skills.	Here's exactly where you started to lose me.
You need to be more responsive.	When I don't hear from you, I worry that we're not on the same page.
You lack strategic thinking.	I'm struggling to understand your plan.
You should do x [in response to a request for feedback].	What do you feel you're struggling with, and what have you done in the past that's worked in a similar situation?

Source: Reprinted by permission of *Harvard Business Review*. (The Right Way to Help Colleagues Excel). From "The Feedback Fallacy" by Marcus Buckingham and Ashley Goodall, issue March-April. Copyright ©2019 by Harvard Business Publishing; all rights reserved.

MAKE IT ACTIONABLE

Thus far, we have focused on part of this mindframe, specifically that you give feedback and work to help receivers understand the feedback. But the other part of this mindframe focuses on seeking feedback yourself. Do you regularly seek feedback? Do you recognize that the feedback offered to you from others will depend on the relationship that they have with you and how much you are trusted? Remember the trust scale from Section 1? That might help you self-assess. In addition, the principal trust survey in Figure 4.3 might be useful in analyzing your beliefs and might just raise some issues for you that you can choose to address such that you receive, and then can act upon, quality feedback.

Figure 4.3 Principal Trust Survey

Directions: This questionnaire is designed to help us gain a better understanding of the quality of relationships in schools. Your answers are confidential.

Please indicate your level of agreement with each of the following statements about your school from **strongly disagree** to **strongly agree**.

	Strongly Disagree	Disagree	Somewhat Disagree	Somewhat Agree	Agree	Strongly Agree
1. Teachers in this school are candid with me.	1	2	3	4	5	6
2. I can count on parents to support the school.	1	2	3	4	5	6
3. Students here really care about the school.	1	2	3	4	5	6
4. I have faith in the integrity of my teachers.	1	2	3	4	5	6
5. Students in this school can be counted on to do their work.	1	2	3	4	5	6
6. I believe in my teachers.	1	2	3	4	5	6
7. Most students in this school are honest.	1	2	3	4	5	6
8. I question the competence of some of my teachers.	1	2	3	4	5	6
9. I am often suspicious of teachers' motives in this school.	1	2	3	4	5	6
10. Most students are able to do the required work.	1	2	3	4	5	6
11. I trust the students in this school.	1	2	3	4	5	6
12. When teachers in this school tell you something, you can believe it.	1	2	3	4	5	6
13. Even in difficult situations, I can depend on my teachers.	1	2	3	4	5	6
14. Parents in this school have integrity.	1	2	3	4	5	6
15. Parents in this school are reliable in their commitments.	1	2	3	4	5	6
16. Most parents openly share information with the school.	1	2	3	4	5	6
17. My teachers typically look out for me.	1	2	3	4	5	6
18. I trust the teachers in this school.	1	2	3	4	5	6
19. Students in this school are reliable.	1	2	3	4	5	6
20. Most parents here have good parenting skills.	1	2	3	4	5	6

Source: Tschannen-Moran, M. & Gareis, C. (2004). Principals' sense of efficacy: Assessing a promising construct. *Journal of Educational Administration*, 42, 573–585.

MINDFRAME 7

I engage as much in dialogue as in monologue.

Having acknowledged that sometimes the school leader must make their expectations clear, the daily operation of the school requires that school leaders engage in more dialogue than monologue. A monologue occurs when the leader tells people what to think or do. During a dialogue, leaders listen and respond, share thinking, ask questions, and work to reach consensus. Garmston and Wellman (1999) describe several ways of talking that occur frequently among professionals. There are two that are relevant here:

ESSENTIAL QUESTION: How can I open up lines of communication with others?

YOUR GOAL: Enact practices that foster dialogue with colleagues.

- *Discussion* is talk that has a purpose—often to make a decision. Discussion may seem unstructured at first as people brainstorm ideas and explore possibilities, but it becomes more structured as people choose sides. It may, in fact, begin to resemble debate.

- *Dialogue* is less structured than discussion. Dialogue engages people in building their understanding of an issue without the pressure to make decisions or be "right." People inquire into ideas, rather than advocate for their own or others' ideas. Doing so builds trust, which is critical to creating a climate in which teachers feel comfortable working.

We consolidate our understanding when we interact with others. As we engage in dialogue, we have an opportunity to extend our thinking and clarify our own understanding. Through interactions with others, our ideas can be challenged and we may come to a new understanding. It is this give-and-take that ensures that ideas are interrogated and understood. In terms of an organization, people need to feel involved and valued if they are going to commit. When school leaders engage in excessive monologues, teachers and other school staff are less likely to feel a sense of ownership in the organization and may not commit as deeply to the mission. When teachers feel involved, through dialogue about important issues, they tend to dedicate themselves to the organization and work to accomplish its goals. School leaders have the *potential* to be magnifiers and multipliers of effective teaching, but it only happens when they engage in more dialogue and less monologue. Some key dialogue skills include the following (www.thinkingcollaborative.com):

- *Pausing:* Take time to listen fully to others before responding.
- *Paraphrasing:* Rephrase what you think you heard and ensure that you understand the perspective of others.
- *Posing questions:* Ask questions to encourage people to share their thinking and to ensure that you understand the thinking of others.

MINDFRAMES

- *Putting ideas on the table:* When you understand others, you can add information to the conversation. Try to focus the conversation on the idea rather than the positional power you have.

- *Providing data:* Give groups information to work with and allow them to draw inferences from the data.

- *Paying attention to self and others:* Notice your emotional state and nonverbal language and ensure that it aligns with your message (everyone else in the group is already noticing).

- *Prompting turn taking:* As a leader a major job is to not let a few dominate, to ensure all feel an opportunity to contribute, and a major predictor of success in developing a strong culture of collective leadership is the amount of turn-taking within any meeting.

- *Presuming positive intentions:* Assume that members of the group want the best for students and are willing to work toward that outcome.

MAKE IT ACTIONABLE

These dialogue skills are important in any circumstance, but especially when it comes to gaining ideas and making decisions about the logistics, structures, instruction, and administration related to distance learning.

NOTE TO SELF

Record, with attendees' permissions, the next team meeting. Notice your moves. Did you pause? Paraphrase? Which of the moves described earlier dominate your style? What do the data say to you about the value you place on dialogue? Use the form below to assess your performance.

	I NEVER DO THIS.	I RARELY DO THIS.	I SOMETIMES DO THIS.	I CONSISTENTLY DO THIS.
Pausing				
Refrain from speaking over others				
Allow time when the speaker finishes before adding information				
Actively listen while others are speaking				
Paraphrasing				
Acknowledge the ideas of others				
Help organize the thinking of others				
Attempt to link speakers' ideas to larger issues				
Posing Questions				
Clarify factual questions when additional information is needed				
Ask questions to elicit additional ideas from the speaker				
Providing Data				
Conversations about data are neutral				
The context of data are discussed				
Discussions remain focused on data				

(Continued)

MINDFRAMES

(Continued)

	I NEVER DO THIS.	I RARELY DO THIS.	I SOMETIMES DO THIS.	I CONSISTENTLY DO THIS.
Putting Ideas on the Table				
Use neutral language to separate data from people or personalities				
Offer ideas to the group for consideration				
Recognize when ideas need to be taken off the table				
Paying Attention to Self and Others				
Monitor my personal reactions to ideas and people				
Monitor my nonverbal behavior to foster social cohesion				
Notice the behavior and actions of others to gain understanding of their emotions				
Presume Positive Intentions				
Reframe statements such that they convey a presumption of positive intentions				
Revisit group norms				
Work to maintain and enhance relational trust				

MINDFRAME 8

I explicitly inform teachers and students what successful impact looks like from the outset.

Some of us remember the goals established by previous U.S. education laws: 100 percent proficiency for all student groups. It's laudable. And it's hard to set policy that does not suggest that all students can achieve greatness. But the punishments for not achieving this level of success caused concern as teachers and leaders were terminated and schools were closed. In addition, some argued that it was not reasonable to expect that level of success in such a short time. Consider a school that had 55 percent of its students achieving mastery. What is reasonable to expect for the next year? When told that they had to achieve 100 percent for all student groups, some stopped trying because they believed that the expectation was unreasonable in the short term.

> **ESSENTIAL QUESTION:** Do all members of the school community know what successful impact looks like?
>
> **YOUR GOAL:** Achieve clarity with expectations.

At the time, progress was not valued. The laws were built on proficiency. And to be clear, we want students to learn a lot. But growth matters as well. Imagine examining the data using both progress and proficiency, as in Figure 4.4. There would be some students who did not achieve well and who made little progress. And others who made a lot progress but not yet to the expected level

---

Figure 4.4 Reading Progress and Achievement

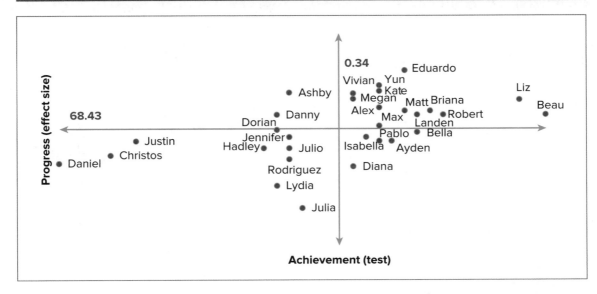

Source: Fisher, D., Frey, N., Almarode, J., Flories, K., & Nagel, D. (2020a). *PLC+: Better decisions and greater impact by design.* Thousand Oaks, CA: Corwin. Used with permission.

MINDFRAMES

of proficiency. And still others who achieved but made little progress. And finally, some who made progress and achieved at the expected level. (Daniel and Diana both started with similar levels of achievement but Diana has made strides in her progress compared to Daniel—merely evaluating your impact on achievement alone would send false messages about your impact on Diana compared to Daniel).

Based on Figure 4.4, what would you expect success the next year (or next unit of instruction) to look like? (In Figure 4.4, the grid lines are the mean achievement and mean progress for this group.) If you say that you expect 100 percent of the students in the upper right quadrant achieving high levels of mastery and making significant progress, you might alienate some of your teachers. Would a 10 percent growth be reasonable? Five percent seems too low. Could you double the achievement of a specific group of students? Who knows? We're not here to tell you what success looks like in your school in the times of COVID-19. But people look to you for direction and they appreciate knowing what the target is.

MAKE IT ACTIONABLE

Part of this mindframe says, "from the outset." There are many opportunities during a school year to inform teachers and students about success. Naturally, we can do so at the start of the year. But what about after a school holiday? What about at the start of a new unit of instruction? How often do you articulate what success looks like?

Start by downloading the progress versus achievement tool from **Visible Learningplus®**, available on our companion website.

You'll need pre and post data to use this tool. You may not have state achievement test data, but what do you have? How will you inform the people you work with about successful impact? What is your plan to inform various stakeholders about the expected impact?

NOTE TO SELF

Plan for communicating expected impact and results to stakeholders.

Leadership

Teachers

Families

Students

MINDFRAMES

I build relationships and trust so that
learning can occur in a place where it is
safe to make mistakes and learn from others.

ESSENTIAL QUESTION: Are mistakes valued as opportunities to learn?

YOUR GOAL: Create a climate in which people take risks to ensure learning occurs.

Let's get real. No one likes to be wrong. When was the last time you failed at doing something and cheerily reminded yourself, "Now I've got an opportunity to learn!" The failure to accomplish something can be demoralizing, especially in the absence of support. However, failure can also be productive, especially when it is followed with further learning and feedback. Imagine if schools were places where errors were celebrated as opportunities to learn. Over time, we might all learn to welcome the opportunities that our errors provide us for learning.

Kapur (2016) describes four possible learning events: *unproductive failure* (unguided problem-solving), *unproductive success* (memorizing an algorithm, without understanding why), *productive failure* (using prior knowledge to figure out a solution, followed by more instruction), and *productive success* (structured problem-solving). Of the four conditions, unproductive failure yields the smallest gains, as the thinking is not guided in any way, and people are just expected to discover what should be learned. Unproductive success is also of limited value, as individuals in this condition rely on memorization only but don't ever get to why and how this is applied. There's just no transfer of knowledge.

Now let's move to the beneficial conditions: productive failure and productive success. Kapur explains that

> The difference between productive failure and productive success is a subtle but an important one. The goal for productive failure is a preparation for learning from subsequent instruction. Thus, it does not matter if students do not achieve successful problem-solving performance initially. In contrast, the goal for productive success is to learn through a successful problem-solving activity itself. (p. 293)

Based on Kapur's model, we identified four possible learning events and their impact.

NOTE TO SELF

FOUR POSSIBLE LEARNING EVENTS

TYPE OF LEARNING EVENT	UNPRODUCTIVE FAILURE	UNPRODUCTIVE SUCCESS	PRODUCTIVE SUCCESS	PRODUCTIVE FAILURE
	Unguided problem solving without further instruction	Rote memorization without conceptual understanding	Guided problem solving using prior knowledge and tasks planned for success	Unsuccessful or suboptimal problem-solving using prior knowledge, followed by further instruction
Learning Outcome	Frustration that leads to abandoning learning	Completion of the task without understanding its purpose or relevance	Consolidation of learning through scaffolded practice	Learning from errors and ensures learners persist in generating and exploring representations and solutions
Useful for			Surface learning of new knowledge firmly anchored to prior knowledge	Deep learning and transfer of knowledge
Undermines	Agency and motivation	Goal setting and willingness to seek challenge		
Promotes			Skill development and concept attainment	Use of cognitive, metacognitive, and affective strategies

Source: Frey, N., Hattie, J., & Fisher, D. (2018). *Developing assessment-capable learners: Maximizing skill, will, and thrill.* Thousand Oaks, CA: Corwin. Used with permission.

MAKE IT ACTIONABLE

We have lost count of the number of times we have heard teachers recording, rerecording, and rerecording videos to make them "perfect" for students. It's causing a lot of stress and it sends the wrong message. As their leader, let them know that they do not need to do this. Mistakes are a natural part of the learning process. Teachers make all kinds of mistakes during physical school and then self-correct. Over time, their students learn that self-correction is a natural part of learning. If every video that students see during distance learning has been scrubbed of errors, young people will miss out on the modeling of self-correction.

In addition, note your own errors and mistakes. Make it known that we are all human, fallible, and vulnerable. Perhaps you would even be willing to share your failure resume?

More recently, there has been attention to the idea of a failure resume. For example, the *New York Times* included an article about this (https://www.nytimes.com/2019/02/03/smarter-living/failure-resume.html) asking if they kept a failure resume, and if not why they should start. As noted in the article, "Failure isn't a roadblock. It's part of the process."

What would be on your failure resume? Take some notes here:

-
-
-
-
-
-

Take a risk and be vulnerable with your colleagues. Start slow, but let them see that you are a complex person who has ups and downs. Let them know you a little more so that you develop the closeness that all humans crave from the adults who teach them. We promise, it will pay dividends. And it gets easier.

MINDFRAME 10

I focus on learning and the language of learning.

ESSENTIAL QUESTION: How can I model the language of learning for staff and students?

YOUR GOAL: Leverage principles of teacher clarity to maintain the focus in distance learning.

Do your students know what they are supposed to be learning? Or do they see the class as a list of things to do? There is a big difference between these two. When students know what they are expected to learn, they are more likely to learn it. Having said that, it's hard to imagine that simply completing a bunch of random tasks will cause learning. If school is reduced to a checklist of things to do, students may complete those tasks without developing a deep understanding of their own learning and the purpose or relevance of that learning. Teacher clarity has an effect size of 0.75. In other words, it's a potential accelerator of student learning. We have organized this into three questions that contribute to teacher clarity, and are answered by three corresponding practices (Fisher, Frey, & Hattie, 2016).

3 Questions That Drive Learners	3 Answers That Accelerate Learning
What am I learning today?	Post and discuss learning intentions
Why am I learning it?	Link learning intentions to relevance
How will I know that I learned it?	Provide success criteria students and teachers can use to gauge progress

For several years, these questions have driven our conversations at the school where three of us work. Throughout the week, we ask students about their learning using this frame and report overall results every Friday in our professional learning session as a way for us to collectively take a temperature check. We don't disaggregate the data by teacher or department, nor do we ask the same students each week. But it has allowed us to detect patterns and trends while keeping the data neutral. We have also had to change the way we ask questions. No more asking a student what they are *doing*. Instead, we ask what they are *learning*. This language has permeated classrooms and students regularly hear the same messages from their teachers.

As we have moved to distance learning, these practices have followed. Distance learning plans for students include each of these elements and are present in each synchronous and asynchronous event. When we virtually visit live sessions, we pose the same three questions to the group, asking them to explain to us what their learning focus is. It continues to be a way to infuse the language of learning with students.

Adults have the same questions in mind whenever they are in a meeting or a professional learning session. It has caused us to be far more intentional about using the language of learning intentions, success criteria, and relevance each time. What's interesting is that we have noticed that formulating each when preparing for a meeting has brought a higher degree of clarity for our own work. After all, if we can't coherently articulate each of these elements, then perhaps the focus of the meeting is incorrect. In some cases, the meeting itself is unnecessary. We are also now including it in our communications with parents about how they can support their children's learning. We invite parents to ask their children the same three questions: *What are you learning today? Why are you learning it? How will you know you have learned it?* During a time when we need to lessen the demand on parents during distance learning, we want at the same time to allow them to focus on what they can do that is truly helpful. Short conversations in the home about learning that is not limited to grades and compliance gives them a way to convey the value of learning.

MAKE IT ACTIONABLE

The language of learning elevates student awareness about their accomplishments and goals. For teachers, it transforms the discussion from a narrow focus on teaching to a deep understanding of the link between learning and impact. We broaden the scope of influence when we assist families in understanding the learning of their children.

MINDFRAMES

Take an account of the ways you foster the language of learning, rather than a narrow focus on teaching or grades, to each of these stakeholder groups. What ideas or initiative can you add?

Ways that students hear the language of learning through schoolwide initiatives	
Ways that teachers hear the language of learning from me	
Ways that families learn about the language of learning	

As we come to the close of this book, we thought a moment of reflection might be in order. None of us wanted COVID-19, and there has been terrible loss around the world. But it is here and it can be a school's Golden Ticket to upgrade to a desired state, such as becoming a Visible Learning school or model. What if this crisis encourages teachers to stop talking so much? Or to not permit students to be so dependent on teachers and instead teach them how to self-regulate and monitor? And what if this leads to students working more with each other to problem solve? Students are more likely to talk to teachers and peers about what they do not know, their confusions, and their thinking aloud at a distance than they do person to person. Teachers can focus the thinking of students and interpret, respond, and evaluate as they invite the student to interpret, respond, and evaluate. COVID has shown that

a. School leaders CAN change schools and quality of outcomes.

b. Educators have remarkable skills and these are most evident in this change and new forms of teaching and learning.

c. Educators can lead and are leading this change (we did not need to wait for administrators or superintendents to mandate change).

d. School leaders can quickly convince parents that the new model is worth bringing back as the new normal.

e. This change leads to new evidence well worth capturing such that we bring schools back better than they were before.

MINDFRAMES

REFERENCES

Bandura, A. (1997). *Self-efficacy: The exercise of control.* New York, NY: W.H. Freeman.

Beaudoin, M. F. (2015). Distance education leadership in the context of digital change. *Quarterly Review of Distance Education, 16*(2), 33–44.

Brown, V. (2019). What we're reading. *Teaching Tolerance, 62.* Retrieved at https://www.tolerance.org/magazine/summer-2019

Bryk, A. S., Sebring, P. B., Allensworth, E., Luppescu, S., & Easton, J. Q. (2010). *Organizing schools for improvement: Lessons from Chicago.* Chicago, IL: University of Chicago Press.

City, E. A., Elmore, R. F., Fiarman, S. E., & Tietel, L. (2009). *Instructional rounds in education: A network approach to improving teaching and learning.* Cambridge, MA: Harvard Education Press.

Clinton, J. (2021). I am an evaluator of my impact on teacher/student learning. In J. Hattie & R. Smith (Eds.), *10 mindframes for leaders: The Visible Learning approach to school success* (pp. 11–22). Thousand Oaks, CA: Corwin.

Clinton, J., & Dawson, G. (2018). Enfranchising the profession through evaluation: A story from Australia. *Teachers and Teaching, 24*(3), 312–327.

Cornelius-White, J. (2007). Learner-centered teacher-student relationships are effective: A meta-analysis. *Review of Educational Research, 77*(1), 113–143.

Covey, S. M. R. (2008). *The speed of trust.* New York, NY: Free Press.

DeFlaminis, J. A., Abdul-Jabbar, M., & Yoak, E. (2016). *Distributed leadership in schools: A practical guide for learning and improvement.* New York, NY: Routledge.

DeWitt, P. (2019). How collective teacher efficacy develops. *Educational Leadership, 76*(9), 31–35.

Donohoo, J. (2013). *Collaborative inquiry for educators. A facilitator's guide to school improvement.* Thousand Oaks, CA: Corwin.

Donohoo, J. (2021). I collaborate with my peers and my teachers about my conceptions of progress and my impact. In J. Hattie & R. Smith (Eds.), *10 mindframes for leaders: The Visible Learning approach to school success* (pp. 35–43). Thousand Oaks, CA: Corwin.

Education Trust. (2019). *If you listen, we will stay: Why teachers of color leave and how to disrupt teacher turnover.* Retrieved from https://edtrustmain.s3.us-east-2.amazonaws.com/wp-content/uploads/2014/09/15140833/If-You-Listen-We-Will-Stay-Why-Teachers-of-Color-Leave-and-How-to-Disrupt-Teacher-Turnover-2019-September.pdf

Education Trust. (2020). *10 questions for equity advocates to ask about distance learning.* Retrieved from https://edtrust.org/resource/10-questions-for-equity-advocates-to-ask-about-distance-learning/

Elliott, K. W., Elliott, J. K., & Spears, S. G. (2018). Teaching on empty. *Principal, 98*(2), 28–29.

Figley, C. R. (2002). Compassion fatigue: Psychotherapists' chronic lack of self-care. *Journal of Clinical Psychology, 58*(11), 1433–1441.

Fiore, D. J. (2000). Positive school cultures: The importance of visible leaders. *Contemporary Education, 71*(2), 11–13.

Fisher, D., Frey, N., Almarode, J., Flories, K., & Nagel, D. (2020a). *PLC+: Better decisions and greater impact by design.* Thousand Oaks, CA: Corwin.

Fisher, D., Frey, N., Almarode, J., Flories, K., & Nagel, D. (2020b). *The PLC+ playbook: A hands-on guide to collectively improving student learning.* Thousand Oaks, CA: Corwin.

Fisher, D., Frey, N., & Hattie, J. (2016). *Visible learning for literacy: Implementing the practices that work best to accelerate student learning.* Thousand Oaks, CA: Corwin.

Fisher, D., Frey, N., & Pumpian, I. (2012). *How to create a culture of achievement in your school and classroom.* Alexandria, VA: ASCD.

Fisher, D., & Frey, N. (2010). *Guided instruction: How to develop confident and successful learners.* Alexandria, VA: ASCD.

Frey, N., Hattie, J., & Fisher, D. (2018). *Developing assessment-capable learners: Maximizing skill, will, and thrill.* Thousand Oaks, CA: Corwin.

Fullan, M. (2019). *Nuance: Leadership for coherence and deep change.* Thousand Oaks, CA: Corwin.

Fullan, M. (2020). I am a change agent and believe all teachers/students can improve. In J. Hattie & R. Smith (Eds.), *10 mindframes for leaders: The Visible Learning approach to success* (pp. 45–52). Thousand Oaks, CA: Corwin.

Garmston, R., & Wellman, B. (1999). *The adaptive school: A sourcebook for developing collaborative groups.* Norwood, MA: Christopher-Gordon.

Garrison, D. R., Anderson, T., & Archer, W. (2000). Critical inquiry in a text-based environment: Computer conferencing in higher education. *The Internet and Higher Education, 2*(2/3), 1–19.

Good, T. L. (1987). Two decades of research on teacher expectations: Findings and future directions. *Journal of Teacher Education, 38*, 32.

Hall, R. M., & Sandler, B. R. (1982). *The classroom climate: A chilly one for women?* Washington, DC: Project on the Status and Education of Women, Association of American Colleges.

Hargreaves, A., & Fullan, M. (2012). *Professional capital: Transforming teaching in every school.* New York, NY: Teachers College Press.

Hattie, J. (2012). *Visible Learning for teachers: Maximizing impact on learning.* Routledge: New York, NY.

Hattie, J. (2020). *Visible Learning effect sizes when schools are closed: What matters and what does not.* Corwin Connect. Retrieved from https://corwin-connect.com/2020/04/visible-learning-effect-sizes-when-schools-are-closed-what-matters-and-what-does-not/

Hattie, J., & Smith, R. (Eds.). (2021). *10 mindframes for leaders: The Visible Learning approach to school success.* Thousand Oaks, CA: Corwin.

Hord, S. M. (1997). *Professional learning communities: Communities of continuous inquiry and improvement.* Austin, TX: Southwest Educational Development Laboratory.

Julian, D. (1997). The utilization of the logic model as a system level planning and evaluation device. *Evaluation and Program Planning, 20*(3), 251–257.

Kapur, M. (2016). Examining productive failure, productive success, unproductive failure, and unproductive success in learning. *Educational Psychologist, 51*(2), 289–299.

Knight, J. (2007). *Instructional coaching: A partnership approach to improving instruction.* Thousand Oaks, CA: Corwin.

Knowles, M. (1970). *The modern practice of adult education.* New York: New York Association Press.

Kosovich, J. L., Hulleman, C. S., Barron, K. E., & Getty, S. (2015). A practical measure of student motivation: Establishing validity evidence for the expectancy-value-cost scale in middle school. *The Journal of Early Adolescence, 35*(5/6), 790–816.

Leana, C. (2011). The missing link in school reform. *Stanford Social Innovation Review, 9*(4), 30–35.

Leithwood, K., Mascall, B., & Strauss, T. (2009) *Distributed leadership according to the evidence.* New York, NY: Routledge.

Manna, P. (2015). *Developing excellent school principals to advance teaching and learning: Considerations for state policy.* New York, NY: The Wallace Foundation.

Martin, A. J. (2013). Goal orientation. In J. Hattie & E. M. Anderman (Eds.), *International guide to student achievement* (pp. 353–355). New York: Routledge.

McNulty, E. J., & Marcus, L. (2020). *Are you leading through the crisis—Or managing the response?* Retrieved from https://leadershipandleaders.com/ceo-role/are-you-leading-through-the-crisis-or-managing-the-response-eric-j-mcnulty/

Mehrabian, A. (1971). *Silent messages.* Belmont, CA: Wadsworth.

Midles, R., & Nichols, K. (2020, April 17). Getting through: Distributed leadership. *Getting Smart.* Retrieved from https://www.gettingsmart.com/2020/04/getting-through-distributive-leadership/

Morrison, M. A. (2019). Reimagined staff development. *Education Digest, 84*(5), 41–45.

Mourão, L. (2018). The role of leadership in the professional development of subordinates. In S. D. Göker (Ed.), *Leadership* (pp. 123–138). Retrieved from https://www.intechopen.com/books/leadership/the-role-of-leadership-in-the-professional-development-of-subordinates

Muhammad, G. (2019). Protest, power, and possibilities: The need for agitation literacies. *Journal of Adolescent & Adult Literacy, 63*(3), 351–355.

Nystrand, M., & Gamoran, A. (1997). The big picture: Language and learning in hundreds of English classrooms. In M. Nystrand, A. Gamoran, R. Karchur, & C. Prendergast (Eds.), *Opening dialogue: Understanding the dynamics of language and learning in the English classroom* (pp. 30–74). New York, NY: Teachers College Press.

Paris, D., & Alim, S. (2017). *Culturally sustaining pedagogies: Teaching and learning for justice in a changing world.* New York, NY: Teachers College Press.

Pfifferling, J., & Gilley, K. (2000). Overcoming compassion fatigue. *Family Practice Management, 7*(4), 39–44.

Reynolds, G. (2008). *Presentation zen: Simple ideas on presentation design and delivery.* Berkeley, CA: New Riders.

Rivero, C. (2020). What teachers need to know. *The Learning Professional, 41*(4), 24–27.

Robinson, V. M. J., Lloyd, C. A., & Rowe, K. J. (2008). The impact of leadership on student outcomes: An analysis of the differential effects of leadership types. *Educational Administration Quarterly, 44*(5), 635–674.

Rosenshine, B. (2008). *Five meanings of direct instruction.* Lincoln, IL: Center on Innovation & Improvement.

Senge, P. M., Cambron-McCabe, N., Lucas, T., Smith, B., & Dutton, J. (2012). *Schools that learn: A fifth discipline resource.* New York, NY: Random House.

Solly, B. (2018, January 24). Distributed leadership explained. *SecEd: The Voice for Secondary Education.* Retrieved from https://www.sec-ed.co.uk/best-practice/distributed-leadership-explained/

Stamm, B. H. (2010). *The Concise ProQOL Manual* (2nd Ed.). Pocatello, ID: ProQOL.org.

Stanovich, K. E. (1986). Matthew effects in reading: Some consequences of individual differences in the acquisition of literacy. *Reading Research Quarterly, 21,* 360–406.

Student Achievement Partners. (2020). *Principles for high-quality standards-aligned professional learning.* Retrieved from https://achievethecore.org/page/3242/principles-for-high-quality-standards-aligned-professional-learning

Sung, E., & Mayer, R. E. (2012). Five facets of social presence in online distance education. *Computers in Human Behavior, 28*(5), 1738–1747.

TNTP. (2018). *The opportunity myth: What students can show us about how school is letting them down—and how to fix it.* New York, NY: Author. Retrieved from https://tntp.org/publications/view/student-experiences/the-opportunity-myth

Tschannen-Moran, M., & Gareis, C. (2004). Principals' sense of efficacy: Assessing a promising construct. *Journal of Educational Administration, 42*, 573–585.

von Frank, V. (2010). Trust matters—for educators, parents, and students. *Tools for Schools, 14*(1), 1–3.

Vygotsky, L. S. (1978). *Mind in society: The development of higher psychological processes.* Cambridge, MA: Harvard University Press.

Wigfield, A., & Eccles, J. S. (2000). Expectancy-value theory of achievement motivation. *Contemporary Educational Psychology, 25*(1), 68–81.

Wiseman, R., Fisher, D., Frey, N., & Hattie, J. (2020). *The distance learning playbook for parents: How to support your child's academic, social, and emotional development in any setting.* Thousand Oaks, CA: Corwin.

INDEX

Douglas Fisher, PhD, is a professor of educational leadership at San Diego State University and a leader at Health Sciences High & Middle College. He has served as a teacher, language development specialist, and administrator in public schools and nonprofit organizations. Doug has engaged in professional learning communities for several decades, building teams that design and implement systems to impact teaching and learning. He has published numerous books on teaching and learning, such as *The Distance Learning Playbook* and the PLC+ series.

Nancy Frey, PhD, is a professor in educational leadership at San Diego State University and a leader at Health Sciences High & Middle College. She has been a special education teacher, reading specialist, and administrator in public schools. Nancy has engaged in professional learning communities as a member and in designing schoolwide systems to improve teaching and learning for all students. She has published numerous books, including *The Distance Learning Playbook, Grades K–12* and *The Distance Learning Playbook for College and University Instruction.*

Dominique Smith, EdD, is a social worker, school administrator, mentor, national trainer for the International Institute on Restorative Practices, and member of Corwin's Visible Learning for Literacy Cadre. He is passionate about creating school cultures that honor students and build their confidence and competence. He is the winner of the National School Safety Award from the School Safety Advocacy Council. He is the coauthor of *Better Than Carrots and Sticks: Restorative Practices for Positive Classroom Management, Engagement by Design,* and *The Teacher Credibility and Collective Efficacy Playbook*, and has written articles for *Principal Leadership, School Leadership,* and *Educational Leadership.*

John Hattie, PhD, is an award-winning education researcher and best-selling author with nearly 30 years of experience examining what works best in student learning and achievement. His research, better known as Visible Learning, is a culmination of nearly 30 years synthesizing more than 1,500 meta-analyses comprising more than 90,000 studies involving over 300 million students around the world. His notable publications include *Visible Learning, Visible Learning for Teachers, Visible Learning and the Science of How We Learn,* and *10 Mindframes for Visible Learning.*

A SAGE Publishing Company

Helping educators make the greatest impact

CORWIN HAS ONE MISSION: to enhance education through intentional professional learning.

We build long-term relationships with our authors, educators, clients, and associations who partner with us to develop and continuously improve the best evidence-based practices that establish and support lifelong learning.

Leadership That Makes an Impact

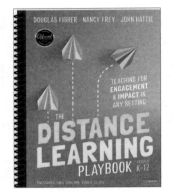

**DOUGLAS FISHER,
NANCY FREY,
JOHN HATTIE**

This book is the essential hands-on guide to preparing and delivering distance learning experiences that are truly effective and impactful.

**ROSALIND WISEMAN,
DOUGLAS FISHER,
NANCY FREY,
JOHN HATTIE**

Share this essential guide with families to help them better support their children and teachers.

**JESSICA DJABRAYAN
HANNIGAN,
JOHN E. HANNIGAN**

This book provides educators with easy ways to incorporate SEL competencies into their virtual lessons and curricula.

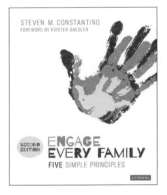

STEVEN M. CONSTANTINO

Join Steven M. Constantino as he shares what he has learned and how he has improved the Five Simple Principles for family engagement and its powerful effects upon student achievement.

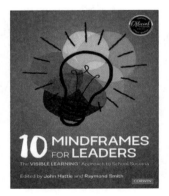

**JOHN HATTIE,
RAYMOND SMITH**

Based on the most current **Visible Learning®** research with contributions from education thought leaders around the world, this book includes practical ideas for leaders to implement high-impact strategies to strengthen entire school cultures and advocate for all students.

**TOM VANDER ARK,
EMILY LIEBTAG**

This inspirational yet practical guide shows educators how to build on students' own talents and interests to develop their desire for a better world, entrepreneurial mindset, and personal leadership skills.

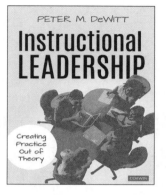

PETER M. DEWITT

This step-by-step how-to guide presents the six driving forces of instructional leadership within a multistage model for implementation, delivering lasting improvement through small collaborative changes.

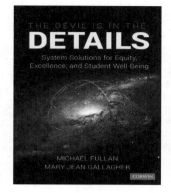

MICHAEL FULLAN, MARY JEAN GALLAGHER

With the goal of transforming the culture of learning to develop greater equity, excellence, and student well-being, this book will help you liberate the system and maintain focus.

CATLIN R. TUCKER, TIFFANY WYCOFF, JASON T. GREEN

Written with system-wide transformation in mind, this is the resource leaders need to help students shift to a blended learning model and transform education for today's learning environment.

JENNIFER SPENCER-IIAMS, JOSH FLOSI

Leading for All is a practical guide that provides a clear pathway for educators to develop a more inclusive school community from start to finish.

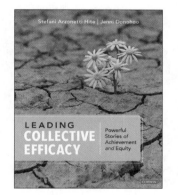

STEFANI ARZONETTI HITE, JENNI DONOHOO

In this book, the authors highlight high-quality professional learning structures and demonstrate how they lead to improved outcomes for both educators and students.

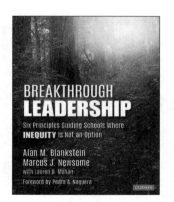

ALAN M. BLANKSTEIN, MARCUS J. NEWSOME

Breakthrough Leadership spotlights professionals now leveraging crises like COVID-19 to shape local and national priorities toward a more equitable and healthy society for our children.